Bringing Spirituality into Your Healing Journey

Bringing Spirituality into Your Healing Journey

ALASTAIR J. CUNNINGHAM

KEY PORTER BOOKS

National Library of Canada Cataloguing in Publication Data

Cunningham, Alastair J. (Alastair James), 1940-
    Bringing spirituality into your healing journey

ISBN 1-55263-450-7

    1. Spiritual healing. I. Title.

BL65.M4C85 2002   291.3'1   C2002-900439-X

The publisher gratefully acknowledges the support of the Canada Council for the Arts and
the Ontario Arts Council for its publishing program.

We acknowledge the financial support of the Government of Canada through the Book
Publishing Industry Development Program (BPIDP) for our publishing activities.

Key Porter Books Limited
70 The Esplanade
Toronto, Ontario
Canada M5E 1R2

www.keyporter.com

Excerpts from *Original Goodness* (by Eknath Easwaran, founder of th eblue Mountain
Center of Mediation, © 1996) are reprinted by permission of Nilgiri Press, Tomales,
California, www.nilgiri.org.
    Portions from the following publications used by permission of *the Foundation FOR A
COURSE IN MIRACLES, Inc.*®, 41397 Buecking Drive, Temecula, CA 92590. All rights reserved.
A Course in Miracles®© 1975, 1992, 1996; *The Song of Prayer*© 1978, 1992, 1996; *A Talk Given
on A COURSE IN MIRACLES*® by Kenneth Wapnick, © 1983, 1989. A Course in Miracles® is a
registered trademark of the Foundation for A COURSE IN MIRACLES®.
    Excerpts from *Goodbye to Guilt*, by G. Jampolsky, 1985, appear by permission of Bantam
Books, a division of Random House, Inc.
    Every effort has been made to obtain permission for the use of material quoted in this
book. The publisher would gratefully accept any additional information on this matter.

Design: Patricia Cavazzini
Electronic formatting: Heidi Palfrey

Printed and bound in Canada

02 03 04 05 06 6 5 4 3 2 1

*This book is dedicated to two wonderful women,
without whom it would not have been written:
my wife, Margaret, for her constant love,
support and wisdom; and Swami Sivananda Radha,
whose inspiring example and patient teaching
showed me what following a spiritual path can mean.*

Acknowledgments

I feel profoundly grateful for the opportunity to write this book and to share with others what I have learned. My gratitude extends first to the Divine Source, for my continuing health, energy and motivation. Closely related is my debt to my wife, Margaret, for her constant support and wise counsel, and to our spiritual teacher, the late Swami Sivananda Radha, of Yasodhara Ashram, British Columbia. The emphasis in this book on personal effort and responsibility derives mainly from Swami Radha's patient teaching and example. Other important sources of growth for me have been attending Self Realization Fellowship meetings (Yogananda), Toronto, and studying A Course in Miracles (Foundation for Inner Peace, USA).

My thanks go to colleagues in our small "Healing Journey" research program at the Ontario Cancer Institute/University Health Network, in Toronto. Dr Claire Edmonds and Dr Cathy Phillips have been excellent associates in clinical and research endeavors, and Ms Jan Ferguson has been a dedicated coordinator of our courses for patients. Among other colleagues of recent years I would especially like to thank Joanne Stephen, Judy Gould, Krista Soots, Sybil Carnell,

Helen Williamson, Leanne Ferreira, Dr David Hedley, Cavell Tyrrell, Dorothy Williams, Kim Watson, Kathy Feher, Rachel Kampf, my secretary, Amy Lee, and Hayman Buwaneswaran, who has set up and maintained our Web site: «www.healingjourney.toronto.on.ca». My daughter, Anne Cunningham, and her husband, Rev. Dr. Barry Moore, kindly read the whole manuscript. Scientific colleagues, superiors, and the medical staff at the Ontario Cancer Institute have maintained their benevolent acceptance of my activities there. Many professionals at the institute have referred patients to our program, and a large number of oncologists have provided assistance with our research on survival. The media have been scrupulously fair in their frequent accounts of our work. And our many patients have shared intimate aspects of their lives as they have struggled to master the crisis of cancer, and to learn what life is truly about. This has been a joint venture—we have all been learning together and continue to do so. My hope is that many readers, whether or not they have a diagnosis of cancer, will also embark on the journey.

Contents

Preface

For most of us, a diagnosis of a life-threatening disease like cancer causes profound distress. As the implications sink in, all aspects of our lives are likely to be affected; we fear for the future, and may experience anger, confusion, sadness, sometimes depression, a sense of futility, and other emotions that degrade the quality of our day-to-day existence. We would like to act, to do something that would make the disease disappear, or at least stop it from progressing, but in health care, unlike most other areas of life, the culturally sanctioned mode of response is still passivity. It is usually assumed that nothing we can do will have much effect on a "physical" disease, and we can rely only on physicians and others to help us.

Nevertheless, there is a growing realization that we may be able to take steps to help ourselves, even in the face of serious disease, and there are now many books on improving health with self-help methods. Some of the best-selling accounts promise near miraculous results for little effort, e.g., through a simple change in diet. They sell because they tell us what we would like to hear. The reality is, of course, far more complex. We *can* help ourselves. We can make a significant difference to our experience, and sometimes to the course of disease, but this requires both time and intelligent effort. In an earlier work, *The Healing Journey*, I tried to present, in a balanced and comprehensive way, an account of this process of helping ourselves through cultivating the resources of our own mind. The present volume is a sequel to *The Healing Journey*. It embodies my own increase in understanding over the ten years since that book was written—an understanding derived from much personal work, and the clinical and research study of many people with cancer.

The focus in this book is on spiritual implications of life-threatening disease, and how we can deliberately strengthen our spiritual connection in the service of healing. When life is threatened by a serious diagnosis we are almost inevitably brought face to face with some of the "big" questions in life: Why did this happen to me? Is there any meaning in it? For that matter, does my life have some meaning, or am I just a genetic accident? Will I somehow continue to exist after my body dies? These are essentially "spiritual" issues, in that they question the existence of an order or dimension that goes beyond the material. These questions have answers, not necessarily in the form of reasoned verbal statements, but as what might be called a "deep knowing." Spirituality is the attempt to make contact with, or become aware of, this dimension of our being. It may emerge from religious belief, or it may have no relationship at all to organized religion.

Why get involved with spirituality as an aid to healing? For two main reasons:

1. *Spiritual work helps us cope with the challenge of disease and to feel much better, perhaps better than we have ever felt, despite the illness.* I have known many cancer patients who have reached this perhaps surprising state of mind.

2. *Strengthening our spiritual connection may modify the biological process of disease.* This is a controversial statement to some, a self-evident truth to others. It is also a notion that extends back through millennia in many cultures. Our technologically oriented culture tends to dismiss the possibility of any significant effect of mind on the body, let alone spirit. Although scientific

evidence is minimal as yet, however, there is increasing support for a potentially healing effect of spiritual connecting, as I will discuss.

Who should read this book?

The writing of this account was driven primarily by an urge to offer help to others, based on what I have learned from my own spiritual practice and exploration over more than twenty years, and from my work with hundreds of cancer patients, trying to help them cope more successfully and to strengthen their spiritual connection. The motivating force feels to me like a strong and loving impulse to share. Of course, there is rational thinking behind it too: a sense that enough has been learned to convey something useful, clinical experience demonstrating the value of spiritual work in coping with crisis, and a judgment that there is a need for a book that specifically targets the use of spiritual work by people with serious illness, and does so in a moderate, responsible way. While *The Healing Journey* ventured into the spiritual, it did so rather cursorily, the main concern being with mind-body techniques. In this book the emphasis is reversed. It can be read alone—and I have provided a chapter recapitulating the main practical points about mind-body healing—but for someone to whom the idea of self-help against disease is completely new, it might be useful to read the earlier work first or in conjunction with this one.

This book has been written primarily for people suffering from life-threatening illness. My clinical experience is almost entirely with cancer patients (a disease that I had myself in 1987), but the principles apply to most other diseases, and indeed to the lives of those who are "well." The book is also relevant to family members caring for or supporting someone who is ill and to healthy people seeking meaning and peace in their lives. There is increasing interest among health professionals in the spiritual dimension of illness. I have kept them in mind also, and trust that they will find that this book helps them to organize or extend their own ideas.

What experience will we draw on?

The spiritual journey is a very personal one, and I will be sharing some of my own experiences throughout this account. I started to take an interest in these matters in 1978, at the age of thirty-eight, through a study of hatha yoga and the philosophy associated with it. I was prompted to do this because of joint pain in my hands. Having seen my father suffer for years from arthritis, I wanted to avoid it. The arthritis abated, but the yoga did more—it introduced me to a realm that I had not known existed: namely that under-lying this material world there is another "deeper" level of reality that we can access through techniques like meditation and reading the writings of "mystics," people who have devoted themselves to experiencing this more fundamental universe. I also learned that we can understand ourselves much more fully than is usual by closely watching our thoughts and reactions to events. This is an insight common to many paths of personal growth, including mod-ern psychology.

I was fortunate, in a world of false prophets, to encounter a gen-uine teacher of unimpeachable integrity, Swami Sivananda Radha, and over a period of years spent many months at her ashram in British Columbia and at workshops given by her or her students. My unfolding awareness of the spiritual reality led to a change in professional activity, away from laboratory research in immunol-ogy, and, after retraining, toward research and clinical practice in psychology. This transformation was supported by my employers and colleagues, to whom I am most grateful. They allowed me to continue at the Ontario Cancer Institute in Toronto but to do entirely different work, developing and researching group thera-pies for people with cancer as well as their family members. Much reading in several of the major world spiritual traditions accompa-nied this change. I explored some of them through workshops and seminars, and my practice of meditation, study, and reflection con-tinue daily. Many, perhaps all, of these traditions and religions pro-vide guidance in healing. However, I am not a scholar in these areas, neither philosopher nor theologian, and I hope professionals in such disciplines will forgive errors of detail. My interest is pragmatic: what can be learned that will help all of us who need help, whether because of cancer, other illness, or simply dissatisfaction with life?

While the substratum for authentic writing about spirituality must be individual experience, there is always the possibility of bias if one relies only on this. Everyone is different. We all experience the world in different ways and have differing talents and abilities to access spiritual connectedness. Thus, the second source of information behind the text of this book is our work with cancer patients at the Ontario Cancer Institute. Several hundred people now attend our clinical programs each year, and many of them choose to wrestle with the spiritual implications of their illness. Many die, of course, but we have seen how prior spiritual work can ease this passage. Others, motivated to work by the threat of death, find a new world opening up to them through their spiritual exploration. As part of our research we have kept detailed notes on people with cancer who have worked intensively with our small team of therapists. We have correlated the degree of "involvement" in this work with longer survival, as I describe in the first chapter. Thus the book draws on what is probably a unique database of systematic clinical and scientific observation of a large number of cancer patients over two decades. Many participants in our programs provided copies of written homework (sometimes amounting to a hundred pages or more). Their thoughts and views are quoted in the book to offer insight and to illustrate points of interest. Though names have been removed to protect their privacy, all quotations are from cancer patients we have worked with.

Although I am a scientist by training, the evidence behind most of the ideas in this volume is not usually "scientific" in the sense of being directly observable by a disinterested third party. Rather, it is "experiential," based on my own direct experience, the reported experience of our patients, and the accounts of many other writers on spirituality. This kind of evidence, if honestly and rigorously observed and reported, may be even more compelling than third-party descriptions. Its validity can be established by the consistency of reports from many individuals, in different eras and cultures. As in psychology generally, in order to describe spiritual experiences we have to rely on people's reported accounts. While moods and feelings, like being filled with joy or sensing that all will be well, are not readily captured by external measurement, the individuals to whom they happen have no doubt about them when they occur. And when we observe that spiritual practices like meditation lead to such experience quite regularly, we know that something important has been documented, as surely as if we measured it on a meter.

Finally, it is important to acknowledge the limits of my own spiritual development. I do not profess to be some kind of enlightened being, simply a sincere and dedicated seeker and observer, with much work still to do. I have personally practiced everything recommended in this book and continue to do much of it on a daily basis. But I can guide the reader only to the boundaries of my own experience and perhaps point the way ahead from there as indicated by the writings of spiritual masters.

What is the "Healing Journey" program?

Our "Healing Journey" program at the Ontario Cancer Institute in Toronto has been constructed in a series of levels or stages, so that people with cancer, and members of their families, can determine how much of the overall program they wish to attend. Everyone begins by coming to four weekly sessions, held in a large classroom, at which they are introduced to some of the basic self-regulation techniques: relaxation, watching the mind, using mental imagery, and setting goals. Many then proceed to the next level, consisting of eight sessions, held partly in a classroom format and partly in small groups (about eight people with a professional leader), in which they can share feelings and experiences. The techniques of the first level are reinforced and extended in the second, and some new methods taught: journaling, meditation, and "Consulting an Inner Healer." (For more details you can look at our Web site: **www.healingjourney.toronto.on.ca**.) Both of these levels have been taught, and their benefits researched, for over fifteen years. "Graduates" with serious cancers have also had available to them a long-term (one-year) therapy group, and a "Life Story" program, in which people with cancer write about their lives and present their stories to a small group.

We have recently offered a course called "Steps Towards Spiritual Healing" for graduates of the second level. The popularity and success of this short course have led directly to the present book. The heart of the "Steps" program is a series of exercises for self-study aimed at diminishing the blocks we all have that hinder direct experience of a spiritual dimension. Teaching this course has reaffirmed for me something that we have learned in all of our courses over the years: change and growth require active study and practice. Relatively little can be achieved by simply reading *about* spirituality. Therefore, the present book is centered around a series of chapters with self-study assignments attached to them, much as in our current spiritual-healing course, but with some additional exercises. As an example, there is a chapter on the tendency we all have to pass judgments on people and events, and assignments that, if conscientiously done, can help us discover the truth of this for ourselves and begin to undo the habit.

The book can thus be used as a text for a discussion group or course on bringing spirituality into healing. This program of active study is introduced by chapters on spirituality and healing, and by a recapitulation of the main techniques of mind-body healing. There is also a final chapter designed for those who have done the exercises and can begin to sense what "healing" ultimately means: discovering, or uncovering, our true identity and how we relate to our world.

Since this book is meant for the thoughtful layperson, the writing here is non-technical, and references are minimal. There is a Reading List at the back of the book. Please view me as a fellow traveler, with ideas and experience that may be useful to you. I trust that the book will prove an introduction and guide to your spiritual self-development, and that it will help you orient yourself as you read other books and try a variety of spiritual and self-awareness techniques.

ALASTAIR CUNNINGHAM
DECEMBER 2001

Part One

Principles of Mind-Body and Spiritual Self-Healing

1 | Spirituality and Its Importance in Healing

What is spirituality?

Since most of us have a rather foggy idea of what "spirituality" means, we need to start with some definitions. Simply put, the spiritual search means trying to gain direct experience of a higher power or order that transcends the material. This order has been given a great variety of names, at different times and in different cultures, e.g., the Universal Mind, the Divine, Brahma, the One, the Tao, the Eternal, Yahweh, and God. To "transcend" means, literally, to rise above or extend beyond, and the implication here is that the non-material spiritual reality not only goes far beyond what we can perceive with our ordinary senses, but also profoundly affects our everyday life. Some people reject this possibility just as, in earlier times, many used to reject the notion that things we could not see caused disease. We have learned to measure and see microorganisms, and we may eventually learn to measure the spiritual. However, the way the spiritual realm acts on our minds and bodies remains mysterious at present. Perhaps there is a precedent now, in our "Age of Information," when we have understood that non-material information encoded in software (basically mathematical programs) can profoundly affect hardware—a factory can be run by such programs, for example.

Is spirituality the same as religion? The words are not synonymous. Religions are institutionalized systems of ritual, faith, and worship, based initially on the spiritual experience of their founders, but not necessarily much concerned with the attempt to gain direct experience of the transcendent. Religious belief may be adopted for cultural and personal reasons, with or without any underlying spiritual experience. A spiritual journey or path, on the other hand, is the process of coming to experience our place in, and our relationship to, a transcendent, non-material order, dimension, matrix, intelligence, or power. The metaphor "journey" captures the essential fact that such experience rarely comes all at once. It takes time and work to realize it. Thus while a religion is an organization within society, spirituality is an attribute of an individual. We may say that religion is about belief and spirituality is about experience, and note that people can be religious without being spiritual, and vice versa.

Another term you may encounter, which refers to the same area of interest, is "mysticism." According to Evelyn Underhill, a famous British writer on the subject, this is "the art of union with reality," and mystics are people whose lives center around this search. The word is widely misunderstood. In the West there is a cultural bias against anything that is "mystical," as opposed to being concrete, straightforward, honest, readily visible, and so on. We will be learning from the great mystics as we proceed. They are, so to speak, the professionals in this field—people who have devoted their lives to understanding and experiencing the divine order.

We need also to distinguish spirituality from "spiritualism" or "spiritism," terms that usually refer to some kind of supposed communication with the dead. And it is important to differentiate between spirituality and emotionality. As the concept of spirituality enters the popular domain there is a tendency to degrade the word "spiritual," and use it for any relatively refined and pleasant perceptions or sensations, such as those evoked by natural surroundings. The label is apt only if the experience evokes a sense of the transcendent.

Healing

The concept of "healing" now needs some discussion. The word comes from the old English "healen," to make whole, and refers to a return to balance and harmony. Medically speaking, healing means restoration of a state where all physiological variables—things like blood pressure, muscle tension, digestion, and the various functions of all organs—lie within a range that is considered "normal." You will see that assumptions are made by this definition, since different states are valued by different people and under different living conditions; e.g., athletes (such as sumo wrestlers) may train their bodies to a state that is outside this range. More important, a medical definition pays little attention to psychological, social, and spiritual aspects of health, registering only extreme deviations in psychological function as abnormal. An expanded definition of healing would attend closely to all of these dimensions, and a truly healed or healthy state, on this view, would include self-acceptance, harmony in a person's interactions with others, and a strong connection with a spiritual matrix.

The body and mind have a great natural capacity to recover from various injuries and to return to balance (as seen, for example, in wound healing, or recovery from psychological trauma). In undertaking a self-directed healing journey we are trying to assist this process with specific methods. Two distinct kinds of action are possible:

- *First we may look for help from **external** sources.* Almost all standard Western medical practices are external modes of help, as is much of what is called "alternative" medicine, i.e., the administration, by an external person or the individual herself, of drugs or procedures (including diet or dietary additives used as treatment).

- *The second kind of self-assisted healing looks **internally**.* It is the deliberate invoking, by the individual, of potentials within his own mind and spirit, e.g., through awareness and changing of thoughts, meditation, mental imaging, setting and pursuing goals, prayer, and so on. We will examine these techniques in more detail in the next chapters. The emphasis in this kind of self-directed healing is on active participation to change states of mind, rather than on manipulating external circumstances.

This book is concerned only with internally assisted healing. This kind of healing forms the basis for the rapidly growing movement of mind-body medicine. We are concerned here particularly with the spiritual dimension and will be presenting a systematic program of techniques and ideas aimed at opening up the mind to spiritual influences, a process that we might call "spiritual self-healing." This should be distinguished from the little-understood phenomenon of "spiritual healing" of one person by or through another; for example, by the "laying on of hands." There are undoubtedly interesting possibilities in such methods, but they are extremely difficult to reproduce reliably. Thus, while we will mention recent experiments on healing at a distance, the book will be concerned with things you can do to help yourself.

Why is the spiritual dimension important in healing?

Modern medicine is highly effective in treating many acute conditions such as bacterial disease or trauma, but becomes much less so as diseases get more serious and chronic. We then enter a domain where spirituality tends to become more and more important, and where it makes sense to attend to all aspects of ourselves and our lives, in the hope that making changes in psychological and spiritual levels may bring peace of mind, and help us to find some meaning in the experience and in our lives. As we will see, it is reasonable to hope also for a degree of physical healing.

The first of these aims, greater peace of mind, is often achieved as people become more spiritually aware, even in the face of life-threatening diseases like advanced cancer. Spiritual techniques like meditation and prayer quieten the mind, reducing anxiety and depression. Contact with a transcendent or divine order can bring reassurance, a sense that, even if death is imminent, all will be well, that this is not "the end," and something of oneself will continue. To the sceptic, this may seem like a fear-induced illusion; to the sufferer it can be a lifeline. Here's what one patient had to say about the effects of her spiritual practice and experience on reducing distress and providing sense of meaning:

> * *I believe that my spiritual work has a very positive effect on my healing. One of the biggest obstacles I have faced to healing has been the stress I have experienced from fear, since I was diagnosed with metastatic cancer. I found that this fear manifested in a number of physical symptoms: tightening in my chest, abdominal discomfort, headache, sleeplessness. I believe that prolonged anxiety affects the ability of my immune system to function, and that the more relaxed and peaceful I feel, the easier it is for my body to heal. I also found that this fear affects my emotional state. It sometimes leads to feelings of sadness, disappointment, anger, resistance, helplessness, etc. The spiritual work I do helps me in both the physical and in the emotional realms. It has helped me to focus outside of my body and physical state, on something bigger than myself. It has given me hope that my life can have purpose, even if my physical abilities are diminished. It has helped me to reach a still, tranquil state of mind, which is useful in dealing with fear. I have learned to accept the range of emotions that come up, and to let them come and go, rather than getting "stuck" in the emotional and related physical states. I think that this is probably better for healing, as the physical effects of stress are reduced.*

This quote also speaks to a second, related benefit of spiritual exploration, that it may generate a sense of meaning and purpose, replacing the despair that serious disease can induce. Spirituality is closely associated with the search for ultimate meaning in one's life. As you can verify for yourself, meaning comes from discovering a relationship to something outside of, and larger than, oneself. We all need to feel that we matter, that our lives have some significance, and usually we seek this reassurance from our relationships with other people, through friends, family and work, and with the natural world. However, when we contract a life-threatening disease, social contact is not enough. Many people ask themselves if this catastrophic event has meaning; that is, did it happen for a reason, does it fit into some overall scheme, or is it just a meaningless accident? Is there some way of knowing that our lives do "matter" in the universe? Does the universe "care" what happens to us, or is it cold and indifferent? Is it, as Albert Einstein pondered, a "friendly place" or not? In spiritual terms, then, finding meaning is about developing an awareness of being part of a larger order or plan, which is often accompanied by a sense that all will be well, even if one dies, and by feeling loved and cared for by God or some higher power. If we are concerned about these questions, we are ready for the spiritual search. Cancer, or some other life event that threatens our safety, can open us up to the quest.

More controversially, it is hoped that spiritual work may actually prolong life. (I describe the available evidence for this on page 37.) To people thoroughly immersed in it, the spiritual journey may become the major focus of their existence, and prolonging life or even improving its quality may cease to be the main concern. Death is simply a stage to be undergone, perhaps signaling the commencement of a new phase of experience. With this orientation, the disease serves as a motivating force to bring attention back to spiritual work as the priority for any time remaining.

As a result of my own experience of cancer in 1987–88, and of being afraid for my life, I became much more attentive and receptive to this universe of meaning and willing to put time into trying to contact it. I had many experiences of feeling loved and cared for by a dimension that I would call God or the Divine. There were some remarkable incidents that might be described as paranormal, but the basic and most important change was uncovering a subterranean river of joy and peace, a sense that all would be well, even if I died, that is still with me, whenever I remember not to be too busily preoccupied with worldly activities. Many others in our cancer-healing groups have had similar experience. I learned that we have to create space for this peace, to pay attention to it if we want to experience it, and that living a spiritual life is a matter of conscious and dedicated attention, which repays the effort many times over. Although I am acutely conscious of my own limitations of understanding and resolve, this sense of spiritual undercurrent has become secure enough for me to take the step of trying to help others find it.

Requirements and obstacles on the spiritual journey

Openness of mind

The most important prerequisite for undertaking the journey is an open mind, a willingness to set aside preconceived ideas and explore for ourselves, using a combination of traditional methods and modern psychological techniques like those that you will find here. I want to emphasize, as strongly as possible, this need for flexibility or open-mindedness. In our research and clinical experience with cancer patients, we have found that many individuals simply do not give themselves a chance to have new experiences because they cling fearfully to fixed and limited notions of what "reality" is, and of what is or is not possible or important for them. This rigidity aborts their progress. A particularly important aspect of this open-mindedness concerns prior and current religious beliefs. Our orientation here is entirely non-sectarian, spiritual rather than religious. If you already have firm ideas that are working for you, I have no wish to contradict them; I want only to challenge you to examine your views. While prior religious experience can help us in our spiritual journey, inflexible religious beliefs can limit progress. For example, rigid concepts of "God" may be stumbling blocks. It is important to remember that the word is not the reality, and that "God" is simply a word. Perhaps it should be viewed as a verb, rather than as a noun. Often, our concepts of "God" are attempts to understand the transcendent by representing it as a human-like figure, albeit a magnificent, perhaps omnipotent one, a sort of idealized parent. This sort of model or picture of the Divine is a "projection" (a term we will discuss in Chapter 7), that is, an attributing of our preconceptions to something we can't fully understand. In many cultures, for example, God has been seen as punitive, reflecting our own guilt and sense that we deserve punishment, which can lead to the view that "I don't deserve spiritual help." So here, perhaps, is your first test of open-mindedness: if you already have a concept of God that you like, are you willing to think about your ideas, how you arrived at them, and whether they still serve you well or need modification? The exercises in Chapters 3 to 11 are useful in deepening our understanding, even for people with long-established religious views.

Another attitude that is common today is that "God" is nonsense, a sort of insurance policy for the weak. If this is your view, you will be able to undertake a spiritual search only if you are willing to suspend scepticism and seek actual experiences. (The exercises at the end of Chapter 3 invite you to engage in an exploration of your current concepts of God.)

To reiterate, please understand that it is not the words, or even the concepts, that matter ultimately; what is important is acquiring the subtle experience of being part of a larger order, a spiritual matrix or dimension, and enjoying all the benefits that flow from this. Although we need words to communicate with one another, they often get in the way. My hope for everyone, whatever your pre-existing beliefs, is that you will find your own way to the Divine and to your own words and concepts to define your experience to yourself. Read the statements below, from two patients who were unable to get past some pre-existing limitations in thinking about spirituality, and from a third who embraced it enthusiastically.

* *I continue to smart from my first experiences with religion. It's very tender and I stay away from things like acts of faith. It has to be demonstrated to me somehow.*

* It feels hypocritical to pray to God only when I am in trouble.

* I feel much more committed to the spiritual work. I sense that a power is working to teach me something and I must stay focused to allow the process to happen. I have no idea of the time frame, but it doesn't matter. The journey is the learning curve.

Willingness to work

Some readers may ask: Why do you emphasize work? Isn't it enough just to pray, or go to church, or ask for help from some divine source? Won't it just happen?

Well no, unfortunately not. Significant progress on a spiritual path requires active work on our part, as sages in all the main traditions tell us. You can choose to see that as a burden or, alternatively, feel glad that there are things you can do to help yourself. Metaphors can help us understand the process of spiritual connecting. For example, taking a healing or spiritual journey is in many ways like learning a new language and familiarizing yourself with the culture behind it: you need to suspend criticism, explore new ideas, and above all, *practice* techniques and ways of being. Or you could imagine yourself as being imprisoned at the bottom of a deep hole in the ground, and that someone throws you a rope. The "rope" in this context is the accumulated wisdom of spiritual seekers from various cultures over several millennia. It is of little use just gazing at the rope, wondering what it's made of, or whether it will support your weight—you need to grab hold and allow yourself to be pulled up, assisting your progress by whatever climbing you are able to do. Trust is required.

In the research I describe below, my colleagues and I found that willingness to work and change was a strong predictor of longer survival. Many of our patients who tended not to outlive medical predictions had an attitude rather like the following:

* I wouldn't be prepared to take six months and do only this self-healing work; the benefits are not sufficiently clear. . . . If there was something

that guaranteed healing I would probably do that all the time, but I'm unwilling to devote eight hours a day on self-help work.

By contrast, those who lived longer than expected had a different attitude, like that of the following patient (alive and well seven years after being diagnosed as incurable):

* *I wake up each morning thinking what I am going to do today for myself (relaxing, meditation, etc.) and when I shall do it. I know it is the most important thing to do in my life at the moment.*

One circumstance that often stops people working is feeling well! Paradoxically, this can be "dangerous to your health," because the motivation is lessened, and it's easier to believe that everything will turn out all right. If, for example, you have had a primary cancer removed, you may just want to return to life as before. Yet this is probably the most effective time at which to do self-help work. Some cancer cells remain in the body after surgery, but the numbers are relatively small, and our regulatory systems (see Chapter 2) have an easier task to control or eliminate these remnants than when cancer is advanced. This is a time for an all-out effort, using healthy mental and physical practices, to help our body's natural healing powers and minimize the chance of a recurrence of disease.

What if you, the reader, are in fair physical health? Is there still healing to be done? Well, of course. Bodies are all subject to gradual deterioration and eventual death. If we continue to see ourselves only as a body, we are likely to become progressively more miserable as aging progresses. On the other hand, if we learn to see our essence as spiritual, the decay of the body-vehicle is much less important. It is perhaps a value judgment to say so, but as Carl Jung, among other thinkers, has pointed out, if we are not engaged in seeking meaning after mid-life, we may be wasting our time. A quote from the great modern sage Paramahansa Yogananda is relevant here: "A person is old only when he refuses to make the effort to change."

How do I become spiritually connected?

Methods of seeking

For the thinking person, the search for direct spiritual experience is best begun with a rational examination of concepts. As these are explored, one's mindset changes to allow new experiences, and we move to a deeper "felt-sense" of what the concepts mean. As an example, in Chapter 4 we look at "judgment." The first task is to recognize the pervasiveness of judging in our mental life (an idea that might be indignantly rejected by someone not willing to do the introspective work) and then to try to diminish this habit. Practicing non-judgment leads to a felt-sense of greater acceptance of others, and ultimately of oneself.

We are responsible for creating the mental receptivity that leads to changes. This work is not about dogmatically imposing or uncritically adopting a set of beliefs. Nor has it much to do with morality. It is rather an investigation, a work-*in* rather than a work-*out*! But as we proceed, we find out that we do not have to do everything alone. There is a spiritual power that helps us. Events seem to unfold as we need them to and "grace" descends. It might be more correct to say we co-create our spiritual state, in much the same way as we co-create, with the artist, a sense of beauty in looking at a picture.

This creation or co-creation has two aspects: The first is removing obstacles, and the second, adopting new practices.

The first is much the more painful, because it involves acknowledging and diminishing ingrained selfish habits, like judgment, guilt, and exaggerated desire. Think of it as removing weeds from your personal garden! Most of the exercises in subsequent chapters are devoted to this end. The second approach corresponds to planting beautiful flowers, which can flourish only in cleared ground. It is, basically, the adoption of habits of thought that connect us with the Divine: "listening" for guidance rather than always seeking control, reading spiritual texts, meditating (which can serve both functions, clearing and planting), adjusting lifestyle to allow time for reflection and meditating, meeting with other seekers, as well as other practices. Note that either approach alone is not enough. We cannot just impose new habits, like daily meditation, on top of a "normal," unexamined, selfish thought-style and hope for significant and lasting spiritual change.

Drawing on established traditions

Modern Western psychology can be helpful in the removal of blocks. In fact, the aim of most psychotherapy is to correct the distorted self-concept, and hence conflict, that many people experience. Thus regular psychotherapy can be a valuable preliminary to the more psycho-spiritual work we are addressing here, and for some people, those with more serious psychological problems, it may be essential. But psychology does not go far enough. It has little to say about the beautiful flowers that we need to cultivate in place of the weeds of conflict that we have removed. For this we need to consult the spiritual masters. If you are new to spirituality, and want to get an impression of these traditional methods, try the "Yoga Sutras" of Patanjali, within the Hindu tradition, or the "Dhammapada" sayings of the Buddha. I offer ideas and quotations from such traditions in this book. Be aware that the language and symbols used often differ from what we are accustomed to (and hence may pose a challenge to our openness of mind). If you are feeling really adventurous, study *A Course in Miracles*—text "channeled" from Jesus in the 1960s. I have drawn heavily on this text, since it is the most profound book on healing and spirituality that I have encountered.

There are, of course, many spiritual paths, many "routes up the mountain," although they share common features and arrive at the same peak. The oldest known system of human spiritual development, yoga, defined by scriptures going back more than 4,000 years, recognizes four main paths, which suit different personalities and cultures:

- the path of understanding
- the path of meditation

- the path of devotion (to God or an avatar—a human who has fully realized his or her oneness with the Divine Order)
- the path of selfless service

As I've indicated, the present introduction to spiritual growth mainly follows the path of understanding, which seems to offer the best chance of relatively rapid transformational change. This is because the power of reasoning is the most highly developed ability in most Western people. Meditation is incorporated and encouraged, however (beginning in Chapter 3), and devotional rituals and ideas are also introduced. Meditation is a vital part of the journey, quietening the mind and helping us to sense our true nature, but understanding is also needed, as insights that emerge during meditation need to be digested and adopted within a growing framework of concepts about reality. A purely devotional path, on the other hand, with its call to surrender to the Divine, is difficult for many Westerners, although a sense of love for the Divine Order develops gradually as we pursue understanding. Selfless service to the Divine (through serving others) is less suited to a person with severe illness, although it becomes more compelling as we heal. We will come back to these concepts in later chapters.

What is the goal of the spiritual path?

The eventual aim of the spiritual path is to arrive beyond the concept of oneself as just a body and mind, and to experience that we are in fact part of God or the Divine Ground, both before and after bodily death. It is a lofty goal, perhaps one whose very desirability is unclear, as yet. All of the great traditions extol, in various ways, this ultimate goal of "God-realization." To a Buddhist there is no separate self, and our work is to drop that misconception. To a Hindu, Atman, the Higher Self within, is part of God, or Brahma. To most Christians, and many Jews, each of us has an immortal soul, and the hope is that through the love of God, we will be resurrected after death.

How is this spiritual search related to the healing journey that many of us are on? In the end, the spiritual and healing journeys are the same. If we are, or have been, ill, we usually begin our search for healing by seeking out support and learning coping strategies, and some degree of management of our thoughts. If we continue, the journey becomes an attempt to find some meaning in the illness experience. As I indicated earlier, in looking for meaning we are asking how the disease is related to all other events in our lives. We come to see that we can't separate them—if one event has meaning, all do.

This investigation of the relationship between all aspects of our lives ultimately becomes a search for our identity. We are asking, "Who am I, really?" Our culture has one answer: that we are entirely separate beings. In the mystical traditions, however, this separateness is an illusion, a creation of our minds; we are, in fact, part of "one mind." Nevertheless, we defend our individuality vigorously, mainly because of the fear of what we might lose if we saw ourselves as merged with something larger. The process of returning to an awareness of unity requires active work because we need to overcome the many obstacles posed by our false conception of separateness. According to the spiritual view, this is the ultimate purpose of our lives. We have to address these obstacles directly. We cannot bypass them and hope simply for enjoyable spiritual experiences, since our psychological views will undermine our capacity for spiritual connection. As Swami Radha puts it in her book, *Kundalini Yoga for the West*: "We need to face ourselves on the gut level."

Where will we end up?

What state of mind may we reasonably hope to reach? An undercurrent of joy; peace; love; "flow"; unity with other people, living things and the Divine are achievable, even if you are facing serious disease. We have seen this in many cancer patients, even in some not far from death. You can expect to get a sense of meaningfulness of events, and that you have a role in the creation of this meaning that will, in turn, confer a satisfying sense of purpose in your own life. If you have cancer, you will perhaps be able to see the disease differently; for example, as a motivator for your spiritual work, even as a "gift." We have often heard this from patients. If you are, or become, well, you will almost certainly want to shape your life toward doing more things that are helpful to other people. In any case, if you are struggling with a disease, the physical problems will become less prominent and the spiritual search more so. "Success" on the spiritual path is evidenced in your state of mind and in your impact on others around you, which can be very great, even if you are dying. To quote from Paramahansa Yogananda again: "Success is when you have so expanded your consciousness that your life is a glory and happiness to yourself and others."

> * *Now that I understand that unconditional love is in me through God who is in me, I want to know, feel, and experience the world as a fully alive person. . . . What I hope to give to others who seek it is a chance for their personhood to be recognized and accepted for what it is.*

> * *On many solitary walks in nature, I have been overwhelmed by the sense that I have not been alone, e.g., a gust of wind on my face, climbing hills, standing or sitting at the peak of a significant pinnacle and reflecting. . . . On this type of "walk-about" I can converse with God in one of the most meaningful/successful ways.*

I have tried to present the essence of the spiritual search in a way that can be used by anyone, regardless of prior religious views, provided they are willing to work conscientiously with their own minds. In this spirit I offer here a theme, or mantra, that would be endorsed by all the main spiritual traditions:

CHOOSE ONLY LOVE.

It is a strategy appropriate for all occasions! Even small progress toward this end brings immense benefits in terms of peace and reassurance. In the working sessions we will practice approaching the world in a non-judgmental way, thus creating an openness through which connection with the Divine may come.

Scientific evidence that spirituality aids healing

An association between spirituality and healing has been consistently noted in diverse cultures and epochs. In spite of the materialistic orientation of our current Western culture and health-care system, this belief and interest persists. I looked up "spirituality and healing" and "healing journey" on the Internet, and found some 300,000 entries for each!

Scientific data is considerably more sparse. There are approximately three hundred articles published in English on the relationship between religion or spirituality and health. Most of these have related simple habits, such as regularity of attendance at a church or synagogue, to better physical or mental health. The physical benefits have included less hypertension, heart disease, or pulmonary emphysema; lowered mortality overall; and better recovery after illness. It is not possible from these studies to conclude that the religious habits are the *cause* of the better health, since it can be argued that, for example, the improved health of those who attend church is attributable to other healthier lifestyle habits. The social support, emotional release of religious practices, and differences in personality between religious or spiritual people and the non-religious might also account for the differences in health. However, expert panels, such as a recent one at the U.S. National Institutes of Health, agree that being religious or spiritual aids health.

There is an intriguing body of experimental data on a related, much more esoteric, group of phenomena: the idea that "laying on of hands," or prayer at a distance (see Chapter 3), or "therapeutic touch," the passage of hands by a healer over a patient, can also promote at least some aspects of good health. Such effects have been shown in animals and even in plants treated by healers. They are widely dismissed by orthodox scientists, as one might expect, although many of the experiments would be quite acceptable if the results were less radical. They are not, however, strictly relevant to our topic, which is the impact of an individual's spiritual qualities on his or her own health.

Perhaps the main difficulty that scientists have with the proposition that spirituality, prayer, or distant, non-physical events might foster healing is that nobody knows how to measure these forces or energies, if that is indeed what they are. Our science cannot account for ways in which a non-material event, connecting with a transcendent reality, could interact with the material or physical world, as represented by our bodies. This does not mean that it is impossible, although that is often concluded, but rather suggests that our theories are currently too narrow to accommodate the phenomena. The truly scientific attitude is to maintain an open mind, look for more factual evidence, and to devise broader theories. A few responsible scientists and clinicians in the health field are currently pursuing this goal.

Does spiritual therapy promote longer life in cancer patients? I have not found any systematic studies dealing specifically with this question (although the anecdotal evidence for an effect of deep meditation on cancer remission, by Meares, mentioned in Chapter 3, is interesting). There are, however, currently about a dozen published studies of fair quality testing the impact of various psychological therapies on the lifespans of people with serious cancers. In much of this work, spiritual or existential issues were discussed as a part of the therapy, but were not a predominant part. Some of these studies have given positive and some negative results. Since *The Healing Journey* was written there have been further negative results. Thus we cannot yet make definite statements about the potential of psychological or spiritual therapy to slow progression of cancer in a majority of patients. One of the problems here has been that investigators have generally adopted the kind of experimental method used to test new drugs: comparing a *group* of patients who received the therapy against a control group who did not. With this design, it is difficult to detect a healing effect in a minority of patients who may have worked hard at helping themselves—their results are lost in the average of the whole group.

Another limitation is that the therapies have generally been rather non-intensive—usually some form of support and encouragement of emotional expression, but without emphasising active self-control techniques. Thus, our current lack of scientific knowledge about the possible influence of either mind or spirituality on healing from cancer result from a small number of studies so far, insufficiently intensive therapy, and experimental designs that conceal the achievements of exceptionally dedicated patients.

How, then, can a scientist justify writing a book advocating spiritual work for cancer patients? Mostly because of my personal experience, and because of clinical observation of the value of spiritual connectedness, made over many years by many therapists, including ourselves. As I've described, spiritual practice generally promotes greater peace of mind, acceptance of difficult conditions, and better quality of life. An association between spirituality and physical healing has been anecdotally noted by therapists, and there are a number of papers on "remarkable survivors" or "spontaneous remissions" of cancer (meaning remissions of unknown cause) where patients have often displayed a strong interest in spirituality. There is one further reason: a unique experiment that we have done, and that we are currently replicating in our own research unit at the Ontario Cancer Institute, Toronto, that I want to describe briefly now.

The reasoning behind this experiment was straightforward: to know whether psychological and spiritual self-help work and growth are associated with living longer, we felt we needed to study, very closely and over a prolonged period of time, a group of people with medically incurable cancer, and to relate what they thought, felt, and did to the duration of their survival. This may seem like common sense, but it is not the way experiments are usually done in medical science, where large randomized trials are the favored method. We had already done one of those trials, with negative results, yet we were convinced from our clinical observations that people highly involved with their self-help often lived much longer than expected (there was even evidence within our trial that a small subgroup who made greater efforts to help themselves lived significantly longer). So we recruited twenty-two people with incurable metastatic cancers of various kinds into our therapy groups. Each patient was free to stay a year in the therapy, and most did so. During this time we asked them to do extensive written assignments at home (much like those in Chapters 3 to 11), and we also made detailed notes of the views they expressed in the therapy discussions. From this mass of records we distilled, with standard methods, a number of psychological qualities, such as "openness to change" and "dedication to self-help work." These qualities were given a numerical rating by a team of psychologists who inspected all the data. We added up all these numbers to obtain a composite index: "involvement in self-help work." We now related degree of involvement to the patients' observed survival; not simply to the number of years lived, but to the extent to which each individual, considered separately, outlived the survival predicted for him or her at the time he or she entered the study. These predictions were made by an expert panel, consisting of fourteen oncologists at our institute who kindly inspected the relevant data from the charts of each patient, and an average of their predictions was taken.

The results were quite dramatic, and highly significant statistically. Being strongly involved in self-help work was associated with living much longer. The one-third of the patients who became most involved in their self-help work generally lived at least three times as long as predicted (two patients had complete remissions of disease lasting seven years at the time of writing), while the one-third at the low end of the "involvement" scale died, on average, at about the predicted time. The remaining subgroup, showing an intermediate level of involvement, lived an intermediate length of time, on average around twice as long as predicted by the expert panel. It was not simply a question of differences in seriousness of disease at the start of the experiment—this was equivalent for the three subgroups. Furthermore, attendance at therapy did not differ significantly between the subgroups—lack of involvement was not, therefore, a result of incapacitating illness. There were other, more sophisticated analyses of the data, which you can read, if you wish, on our Web site: «www.healingjourney.toronto.on.ca». The most probable conclusion appears to be that getting involved in helping yourself psychologically and spiritually prolongs life. Technically speaking, the differences in survival could conceivably be due to other factors, but it is very difficult to see what these might be. It is also not possible to say for sure that spirituality was critical, but we observed that it was very important to all in the top third, while there was very little such interest among the bottom third.

I hope this is encouraging to cancer patients and members of their families reading this account. The experiment confirmed what my team and I had been observing for many years, and our current work with further patients is tending in the same direction, although it will not be complete for some years yet. You should know, however, that the mainstream medical research community is little moved by such an experiment. While our initial results have been published, they were rejected by the two prominent medical journals to which we sent them at first. To a physician or other professional who has been educated in the philosophy that only material means will affect physical diseases, and who has not worked with large numbers of patients interested in helping themselves, it will take much more than this experiment to change his or her views. This is not unusual in science. For very many years, technical and statistical arguments were levelled against the idea that smoking causes lung cancer, until the evidence became overwhelming. Much the same process will have to be gone through, I believe, with healing through mind and spirit. Meanwhile, people are getting cancer and are looking to help themselves. It is left to the individual reader to decide whether the case for physical healing is sufficiently compelling at this point to provoke his or her interest, or whether the undisputed quality of life benefits that come from spiritual connecting warrant active involvement in this kind of work.

2 | Mind-Body Healing: The Basic Techniques

Before we begin the practical work of trying to strengthen our spiritual connectedness, I want to review the main principles of mind-body healing. In this chapter I first provide a brief justification for the mind-body approach to healing and then describe the basic techniques that we need to learn as a preliminary to our spiritual work. This introductory material has been covered in more detail in *The Healing Journey*, and the techniques are used by many therapists, so you will also find them, or variations on them, described in books listed in the Reading List.

Why is it reasonable to expect that the mind can influence physical healing?

Since we live in a culture that sharply separates mind and body, we need to explain how our minds affect our health. First, we all know that our behaviors are important in maintaining health, e.g., not smoking, eating wisely, and getting adequate exercise and rest. I will assume that these principles are known to readers (even if there is sometimes a divergence between our awareness and our actions!). The view that the mind can affect the course of an existing illness, however, and particularly cancer, is more controversial. Let's look at why cancers develop, then at the possible influence of mind on their progression.

Cancers develop for two main reasons:

1. *Random changes or mistakes occur in the DNA (the genetic material) of cells as they divide.* These mutations may be provoked by external agents, like the carcinogens (cancer-producing agents) in tobacco smoke, or they may have no known cause. Certain kinds of mutation give rise to potentially cancerous cells, which may then divide repeatedly to yield a dangerous mass.

2. *There is inadequate control of these repeated cell divisions.* All dividing cells are regulated by a series of messenger molecules in the tissues, but if this system of regulators is somehow deficient, potentially cancerous cells, which are present in everyone, are more liable to grow into clinically detectable cancers. Although this regulation is not well understood even after decades of research (because it is so complex), there is a lot of evidence that it exists. For example, when breast or prostate tissue is examined at autopsy of people who have died from causes other than cancer, the pathologists find small pre-cancerous lesions or nodules far more frequently than would be expected if all of these were inevitably going to grow into full-fledged cancers, pointing to effective control of potential cancers in most people.

Our minds influence both causes of cancer. We can influence the probability of mutations by opting for more healthy behaviors—not smoking, choosing a healthy diet, and adopting other healthy habits such as moderating our exposure to sunlight. Once we have a clinical cancer, however, we can't reverse the mutations but may address the second reason for cancer progression, that it grows because of a failure of the body to regulate or control it. We need to strengthen the mechanisms that regulate cell growth.

How? Eventually we may know enough to do it by injection of chemical agents that make the normal controls in the body work more efficiently. For the present, we don't know how to do this, but we do know something that will help us, which is a central idea in this book: **We know that the mind, or the brain, is the master regulator in the body.** We can work with our minds to improve conditions in the body so that the cancer meets more resistance to developing and growing.

The mind/brain has an effect on almost everything that happens in the body, through two pathways: the nervous system and the endocrine, or hormonal, system. There is an elaborate network of nerves spreading from the brain and spinal cord that penetrates into and influences virtually all the organs in the body. And the brain, through the pituitary gland directly underneath it, and by other routes as well, sends chemical and nerve signals to the adrenals, the pancreas, the gonads (sex glands) the thyroid and parathyroid, the thymus, and lymph nodes, all small organs that in turn produce a second wave of messages and cells that carry out the "instructions," so to speak, of the brain. If those instructions are to promote harmony and balance in the body, then the nervous system and endocrine system will endeavor to carry out that plan. One particular pathway that is well documented is the effect of the mind/brain on the immune system. Mental perception of stress can significantly diminish the power of the body to make an immune response, which in turn may weaken defenses against certain cancers.

This may all seem a bit technical. I explain it in more detail in *The Healing Journey*, but you could think of it like this: cancers usually take years to develop to a size where they become detectable. When they are finally found, they have grown very accustomed to the chemical environment or "soup" that your body provides. If you are an angry person, they have grown to tolerate angry soup. If you tend to be depressed, any cancer that grows to visible size tolerates depressed soup. In order to change its rate of growth from the inside, and so help your body resist the growth of cancer, there must be changes in the soup. The direction of those changes is toward harmony, peace, relaxation, and absence of undue stress and conflict. As the mind changes in this way, it will signal the body that all is well, and the soup will return to a composition that is the best possible for healing and restraining cancer growth.

The same principles hold for many chronic diseases. The body has many mechanisms for maintaining its equilibrium in the face of a multitude of challenges from outside. Think, for example, of the way our body temperature is maintained within a narrow range, in spite of wide variations in surrounding conditions, or how blood pressure is held relatively constant. By consciously trying to live in harmony within ourselves and with our environment we provide the best internal environment for restoration of health.

Healing as a journey

When people consider how they can assist their healing, the initial hope is often that some simple remedy, or perhaps a trick of the mind, will prove effective. Many popular books and irresponsible therapists promote such simplistic "remedies," and this is partly why alternative medicine has gained a bad reputation in medical circles. In fact, self-mediated, or mind-mediated healing is a process that takes time and effort. If you think about it, how could it be otherwise? Any simple material remedies, if effective, would already be part of the regular treatment repertoire.

While everyone is a little different, there are common features in people's journeys, which tend to have three main stages, as shown in the "map" below (Figure 2.1). The first stage we may call "taking control." In this phase, having acknowledged the seriousness of a threat to health (without which there is unlikely to be motivation for change), the person learns certain basic self-control strategies. These continue into the second stage, "getting connected," where the emphasis shifts toward understanding how one's mind works and getting to know the old, established patterns, many of which

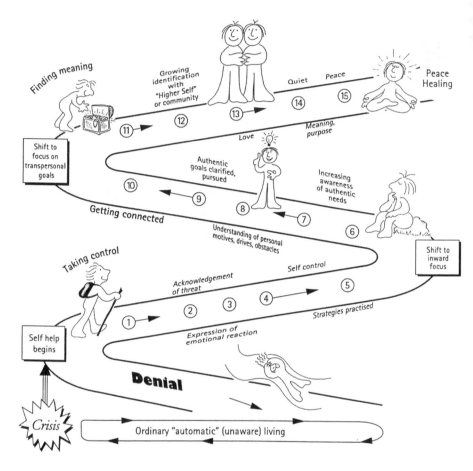

Figure 2.1
The healing journey.

hold us back. Then the third stage, "finding meaning," is about discovering how we fit into a larger, spiritual reality. The present chapter recapitulates the methods of the first stage. The bulk of the book, however, is a combination of the second and third stages: understanding the psychological blocks to spiritual connection and learning techniques for enhancing spiritual experience.

Connecting the many levels

Next, have a look at the "Connectedness" diagram (Figure 2.2), which also appears in *The Healing Journey*. It has proved very useful in helping people organize their self-help efforts. It is another map, this time of a person, showing that we have not only a body, but also several other dimensions. There's our conscious mind, or stream of thoughts. Then there's what we can call the "deeper mind," which includes our emotions, our imagery, and all the buried ideas and fears that may never come to our awareness, but that influence our actions all the same (more about all this later). Those are the first three rings in the diagram. The fourth ring is "social," indicating that we all belong to some society of people and couldn't exist without them—so, in a sense, we each contain part of this social organization. And, finally, there is the existential or spiritual dimension.

The old-fashioned view of cancer, still prevalent in some medical circles, is that it is purely a genetic accident in the body (represented by the small mass, A, in the diagram). The newer view, which takes into account the biological research that I outlined above, is that factors at all levels may contribute to development of cancer by affecting regulation at the tissue level. I have shown this as a kind of "party balloon," B in the diagram. It presents the idea that we can intervene at all of these levels to help our bodies fight the cancer. Think of it as sticking a pin into the balloon at any level!

The diagram helps us see what we have to do, to organize our self-help work. We need to connect with all of these dimensions or levels of ourselves. To "connect" means to become aware of what is happening and what needs to happen at each level, then to supply that need. As this process gets stronger we move closer to a state of balance or harmony.

The social level
Let's start with this, since the ideas are quite familiar to most people. The important principle is "Communicate." And the first person to communicate honestly with is yourself!

CONNECTEDNESS

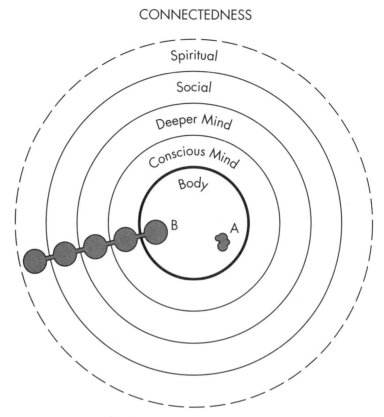

Figure 2.2
Cancer affects us at many levels, so we approach healing at many levels.

We begin taking control by looking honestly at our situation. Is our life under threat? Most kinds of cancer do pose a threat, although it varies greatly with the site where the cancer begins and the extent to which it has grown and spread. So are we willing to acknowledge this threat, or do we prefer to say to ourselves "the doctor got it all; it won't come back; it won't spread further, not in *my* body"? The problem with these kinds of reassuring self-statements is that they may prevent us from taking helpful action. It's not that we want to be living in constant fearfulness, just that we need to be realistic about what is happening.

Having acknowledged to yourself what is really happening, be equally honest about how it makes you feel. It helps greatly to talk to others about this. There will be times when we are scared, or depressed; perhaps times when we feel angry. These feelings are normal—a normal reaction to an overwhelming challenge. So please don't blame yourself for having them, and don't just bottle up these feelings. We don't really need to protect others around us. In fact it's a lot more respectful of them to say how we truly feel.

If you can talk to your family, do so. Make time, when nobody is rushed. Discuss what will happen if you die. Many couples never do this, but it needs to be brought out into the open, and you will all feel more comfortable, eventually, if you do. Of course with young children a somewhat different approach may be needed, but it is still helpful to be honest about what is going on, otherwise they may get all kinds of strange ideas, such as that they somehow "caused" your illness. Other people may find it difficult to cope with the relatively sudden changes they see in you that this life-threatening disease has induced. Be prepared to reassure them and tell them what you need from them. For example, it might be appropriate to say, "I know I'm less tolerant these days because I'm worried about the cancer, but I value your company and support." If your family refuses to hear how you feel or insists on being "positive" all the time, you may instead find a friend to whom you can talk freely. It's an excellent idea to attend a support group, a small discussion group with perhaps six to ten members. It's usually better to attend one that is led by an experienced professional. However, if you live in the country, or are otherwise away from such services, you might try getting a group of like-minded people together to talk.

Apart from sharing with others how you feel about the cancer, we all need the friendship and support of others. Seek out those people who make you feel comfortable and appreciated, and avoid others who do the reverse. It is appropriate to avoid more superficial, perhaps stressful social interactions, and to favor those that are meaningful to you, like heart-to-heart conversations with old friends.

Communicating with other people in order to learn more about myself, share my knowledge, and learn about things that interest me is important to me. Through this process, I will understand more about myself, help others with my experience and knowledge, and learn about how the world really is. . . . In addition I am expanding my ability to forgive myself and people around me, which is giving me the ability to communicate with and learn more about who these people really are (i.e., becoming more perceptive as the need for control goes away). The process of becoming is very exciting. I have yet to figure out what job(s) will suit me in the future, but I trust that will become clearer as I go along.

Body level

When people think about this level they frequently wonder first if special diets can have value for their healing. Briefly, it is important for general health to eat well (which often means some changes to our habits), but there is no evidence that the extreme diets advocated in some quarters make any difference to an existing cancer. There is no rational reason, for example, to avoid all meat, dairy, sugar, processed flour, coffee, and alcohol, which is the advice that some of our patients have received from various sources. In fact, there is good reason not to take these draconian measures: life can seem less worthwhile if you do, and you can be a considerable nuisance to the people around you!

To judge the value of unconventional diets or other remedies, you should ask yourself three questions:

1. *Is there **evidence** that it works?* Ensure these are not just claims—claims are easy to make—but documented evidence. Find out how many people tried it. What kinds of cancer did they have? For how many did it "work," i.e., cause a remission? Most important, for how many did it *not* work? (This we are rarely told!)

2. *Is there a **rationale** for how it works?* In other words, is there a plausible mechanism by which this remedy could work, one that makes sense to people able to judge?

3. *Is there **consensus** that it works?* This consensus should be among people with relevant experience and no vested interest in promoting it.

Unfortunately, many unconventional remedies generally fail all three tests. While they may have some value of inspiring hope, the same hope can be generated by adopting rational, psychological, and spiritual self-healing methods. For these there is considerable evidence of effectiveness, a rationale (for example, the improvement of immune function by controlling stress, as I described earlier), and consensus among professionals who have studied these methods (which includes some, but not all, physicians).

The most basic and important new technique to learn at the body level is deep relaxation; not the kind of relaxation that comes from a pleasant or undemanding activity, like reading a novel, but a deliberate process of releasing tension in your main muscle groups. This produces a state of mind that most people have never experienced, in which the mind also becomes very quiet and peaceful.

Methods of Relaxation

There are various ways to relax. We always start by closing the eyes and focusing our attention closely on breathing for a minute or two. Then we might use "progressive muscle relaxation," which involves tensing and then relaxing all the main muscle groups of the body, one after another, so that we end up with all of them relaxed to a much greater degree than usual. Or we may slowly scan through the body in our imagination, noting whatever feelings of pressure, tightness, discomfort, or other indications of tension we find in each region, and then "letting that go," "breathing it out," or imagining relaxing energy flowing through the area.

Once we have begun to relax the muscles, we can deepen the relaxation by imagining going down a flight of stairs or, better, being carried down on an escalator, relaxing further as we go. We may end up in a "healing room," which we furnish in our imagination, putting a big recliner chair somewhere within it, and we go to this chair and sink down into it, letting any remaining tension drain away. Or, alternatively, we can, following the initial muscle relaxation, take an imaginary trip to the beach (or to a garden, or chapel, or cottage, or any other place we associate with our own relaxation and peace of mind), then paint a detailed mental picture of that place and imagine being there, as intensely as we can. The body, which does not know the difference between "real" and "imaginary," will act as if it were there and relax profoundly.

These techniques are best learned with the aid of a teacher/therapist or an audiotape. You can get our relaxation tapes in the package "Helping Yourself" from the Canadian Cancer Society (see the list of Further Readings at the end of this book). Many other relaxation tapes are also commercially available.

Learning to relax deliberately is the absolute bedrock technique for healing through the mind. It is immensely valuable in itself because it gets your mind and body into a quiet state conducive to healing. Furthermore, we can't do much in the way of imagery or meditation without some ability to relax. So please do find yourself a tape that you like and practice daily until you become reasonably proficient. It is a good idea to have a regular time each day at which you practice; that may save you from the constant negotiation—will I do it now or later?—which can otherwise lead to missing sessions and finally abandoning it altogether. You'll need to explain to your family what you are doing, and make the time and space (in private) for yourself. Put the cat out and take the phone off the hook! A big reclining chair is perhaps the best support for learning.

  * I can let my body relax by thinking about the relaxing and letting go.
  I do this when I think of it—it makes my mind think about itself and
  I try to slow things down. If I do this often enough and long enough
  I generally feel quieter—I sleep better at night. The more you relax
  your body the faster your body learns to "let go." I can sit quietly and

take a few breaths and relax while breathing out and then think about my left arm and my body relaxes.

* *While I'm sitting, I have changed the focus of my relaxation and meditation somewhat. I often start with a body scan, some breathing meditation (noticing thoughts, images, and feelings), and then I visualize white, warm energy/light traveling through my head and into each part of my body. I feel the physical sensation of energy flowing. I give thanks to God for sending this healing energy and I imagine it flowing out and through other people I love. I think about the many signs of divine presence I have noticed each day and give thanks. If I have trouble visualizing this healing light and energy (sometimes it comes more easily than others), then I try affirmations such as "God's warm, healing energy is flowing through my chest," etc.*

There are many more sophisticated techniques that aim to connect mind and body, that is, to bring into your mind more awareness of how your thoughts are influencing your body in subtle ways. For example, yoga and tai chi are available in most cities these days. I have had experience with both, and they are powerful, and can in fact take you a long way on a spiritual path by themselves, if intensely pursued. Chi gong (Qi gong) is said to be good also. But for the purpose of establishing a basis for your spiritual work, learning to relax well will be enough at first.

Conscious mind
Getting acquainted with our thoughts A stream of thoughts is passing through our minds most of the time, often without our being aware of most of them. Yet these thoughts define what we experience. For example, we may walk into the doctor's office feeling fairly well and not unhappy with life and walk out an hour or two later, having been diagnosed with cancer, feeling desperate and hopeless. Nothing has changed materially, except for the thoughts in our minds. In other words, it's not usually the cancer itself, or events in general, that make us depressed, it's our thoughts about them, what we think they imply.

It is fundamental to self-healing to become conversant with our thoughts. Most people, I have found, have surprisingly little awareness of what they are thinking (I didn't either until I began watching my mind about twenty-five years ago). Without this, we cannot change, and changes in all aspects of our lives usually start with our thinking. How can we gain this awareness? A good first exercise is simply to sit quietly for ten minutes or so, eyes closed, and "watch" your thoughts. You may feel that you have an "observer" in the back of your head who watches with interest. Then at the end of this period (use a timer if it helps), write down the main ideas that you can remember passing through your mind.

"Know thyself" said the Oracle at Delphi, over 2000 years ago, and we know ourselves, initially, by being aware of our thoughts, which define who we think we are. So if you want to know yourself, which is the first step in healing through the mind, please *don't skip* this little exercise. Instead, do it many times, until it becomes a habit to monitor your thoughts as you go about your daily round. If you are one of those stern, tightly controlled types who say, "My mind is naturally quiet; I don't notice any thoughts when I sit with my eyes closed," then you are almost certainly not catching them and need to relax a little and observe more closely. And don't worry that this practice will interfere with your actions or your spontaneity—it will in fact free you from much of the automatic behavior that is driven by unrecognized thoughts and emotions.

What do we discover when we watch our thoughts? For most people, there's a torrent of ideas, impressions, and reactions, with the mind jumping about from one thing to another, largely out of control. If we liken the mind to water, then in our usual state it resembles a muddy torrent, rushing down a hillside, and carrying all before it: rocks, trees, and other debris. Sometimes it gets fixed in one channel, roaring on with a will of its own, and it may be very difficult to stop this, as when we worry about what might happen because of disease. Wouldn't we rather have the mind like a still lake, calm, serene (at least most of the time)? Meditation is essentially clearing the mind, letting the mud settle, so to speak. When it's still we can see down into the depths; if the surface is choppy, we can't see beyond that. Furthermore, our bodies adjust to our thinking, and if we are in a state of constant (usually unpleasant) arousal, a great deal of energy is wasted, energy that we need to fight the cancer. Constant aimless thinking, even when it is not fearful, wastes energy in this way.

So the initial discovery is likely to be chastening; the content of our minds is not very elevated! In fact, it tends to be full of fears or anxieties, resentments and judgments, replaying of old grievances, compulsive planning for the future. Acknowledging this to ourselves is a good start.

What else will we find out as we monitor our thinking? It begins to dawn on us that thinking is a voluntary act—we don't *have* to think! We do not need to be slaves to our unruly minds, tyrannized by uncontrolled thoughts. It follows from this that we can exercise some choice in what we allow or put into our minds. Our minds function at the level of what we put into them. Unfortunately we are surrounded by "junk thoughts"—in the media, in superficial interactions with others—so we need to be vigilant if we are going to refine our own processes.

Another discovery we will make is that a close bond exists between thoughts and emotions; essentially all emotions are preceded by a thought (check this out for yourself). Sometimes the transition to emotion is very fast, but if you are feeling afraid or angry, backtrack a bit, and you will find the ideas that led to that feeling. This is important because it gives us a powerful means of control over our emotions. Once a strong emotion has taken hold, it is very difficult to change, but if we catch our thinking early enough we can stop the feeling from developing, or modify its expression.

Managing our thoughts We can now set down a series of steps in exercising some control over our thinking, steps that are particularly valuable when we are faced with serious disease, and when our thoughts tend to become exaggerated or irrational. An example, familiar to most people with cancer, is that every little ache or pain means "my cancer is spreading!"

Step One: find out and acknowledge to yourself what you are thinking.

Step Two: acknowledge what you are feeling and determine how it is related to your thoughts.

Step Three: express the emotion appropriately. If we are very depressed or angry, we need to express this in some way, as in the old sayings "letting off steam" or "getting something off our chest." The best way is usually to talk to someone else. Other ways to let out emotions are writing in a journal; going for a long walk or taking other exercise, while consciously "letting it go"; using music to match and express your mood; bashing a pillow with a bat or racquet to let out anger; and driving with the windows of the car up so that you can yell or scream (one of the few places where we can do this).

Step Four: changing the thoughts. This will usually mean substituting a more positive, optimistic, or life-affirming idea for the old depressing one. For example, if a thought that keeps going round and round in the head is, "I've got cancer and I'm going to die," you might, having acknowledged it and allowed yourself to experience and let out some of the fear, substitute, "Today I am well, and I am going to enjoy every minute of this day"; or, "I am doing everything I know to oppose this cancer"; or, "This discomfort means my body is fighting the cancer; I am optimistic and strong." You will probably find that you need to do this whole process many times, to "fight it out" with your own thoughts. It is hard work, but it does work. If you think you can't do it, consider the focus you are able to bring to bear in other areas of your life, for example, on a hobby or a sport, or recall your first romantic love interest—was concentration a problem there?

* *I've observed the connection between the thoughts I've been having and the emotions I feel. I try to sit with the feelings, noticing how they affect my body, having faith that they will pass. I imagine a healing light around me, which I can breathe into my body. Painting helps me to relax and to get out of my obsessive anxiety thoughts. Daily prayers where I focus on things that I am thankful for and feelings of love for friends and family are helpful. Crying seems to help relieve the*

stressful feelings, so I can do some of the other things listed above. But each day I do my prayers, meditation, and visualization, and it restores my hope. During these times I sometimes find it very hard to sit with feelings of sadness, discouragement, etc. When this happens I try to tell myself that it will pass—and eventually it does.

* *For the last few months, I have had sporadic pain in the left side of my back [rib area]. Over the last two weeks, the pain has become quite regular, i.e., daily. This, of course, makes me think that the cancer has spread to this area. I know that cancer patients often react to any new pain, discomfort, or change in their body as a sign that the cancer has spread. . . . I asked myself, "If this were true, what would it mean to me?" This exercise was useful. It helped me to be aware that my underlyng concern is going back into more treatment. Being aware that this was the worst of my fears, I was less tense and anxious when I thought about the pain.*

I [also] became keenly aware of how readily I have an internal monologue about the appearance of others. I was constantly critiquing other's clothes, body shapes, actions, and speech. I thought a great deal about how easily I "label" people. I don't even know them, but I am ready to place a label on them based on my immediate reaction to what I see or hear and my preconceived notion as to what that means to me.

After a while, I was able to consider the endless body shapes that God has created, the beauty of so many people, and the fact that a number of people no doubt had negative thoughts about my appearance. If I am happy with my appearance, I am sure that most of the people I internalized about are quite happy with both their choice of clothes and their bodies. I observed others differently, instead of grabbing on to what I perceived as the slightest weakness or flaw in someone and generalizing it as a character trait or bad choice on their part. I learned that hesitating and delaying judgment was better than rapid judgment.

There is plenty of scientific evidence for the value of such thought changing, which is now widely used as a therapy for depression. It is important, however, not to expect magical effects. For example, just telling yourself that "the cancer will be gone tomorrow" will lead only to disillusionment. Your deliberate thoughts should be realistic, e.g., "My defense system is attacking my cancer." They should also be simple, and direct, without negatives. For example, if you say to yourself, "I will not succumb to the cancer," your deeper mind might miss the "not"!

People label some thoughts as negative and others as positive. It's not really an accurate description; unpleasant and pleasant is usually what's meant. There are no negative thoughts, just thoughts—the whole range of ideas and emotions are equally part of who we are. It has been said that the only bad emotion is a stuck emotion, the point being not to become fixed in any one emotional state, but to let the feelings flow through you, so to speak, then to dissipate, leaving space for the next set. It is important not to think that having occasional negative (pessimistic) thoughts is somehow a failure, or dangerous to our health. Rather, it is our *habitual* thinking patterns that matter. Allowing constant anxious or depressing thoughts to take over our minds is going to produce a corresponding mood and have an effect on our bodies. Note also that simply avoiding anxiety-producing thoughts, without first acknowledging them and dealing with them in the way I've described is not a helpful strategy in the long run. The thoughts and emotions then stay in your mind, and may break out in other ways later. We need to face what we are thinking and experiencing, and to tolerate the initial discomfort of doing so, if we are to make significant change.

Deeper Mind

Emotional management The "deeper mind" is a non-technical term, intended to include our emotions, our imagery, our dreams, and those ideas and impulses that we are not aware of, but that influence much of our normal conscious life. As we have seen, our thoughts affect our emotions, and thus every part of our lives; the conscious and deeper mind levels overlap here. We have talked a bit about the great importance of sharing our emotions with people who are prepared to listen. This moves the emotion out of the deeper mind, into conscious awareness, and eventually "discharges" at least some of it. That's a metaphor of course, but it is how it feels. Everything we do in our healing journey affects mood: our imagery, which we will come to in a moment, our awareness of the impulses that drive us, and our spiritual connectedness. It would be fair to say that mood, or emotional state, is one barometer indicating the degree of balance or harmony in our lives. The aim of the journey is to reach a state of fairly constant, calm joyfulness, which can happen only when we are not tossed around by uncontrolled thoughts and desires.

Mental imaging There are two main pathways by which our mind controls the reaction of our bodies to the environment. The first is through thoughts, the second via imagery. The following diagram (Figure 2.3) shows this. The two are connected—thoughts and emotions inspire images, and vice versa. Imagery is really a language, and a much more primitive one than words. Our ancestors must have relied on it almost exclusively during most of the evolution of our species, so we will not be surprised to find that it has in some ways much more power over the body than words do. In learning to focus our imagery we are not simply acquiring some kind of mental trick or technique, but rather taking some control over this parallel language, one that our mind uses constantly to communicate internally, and with the body.

Images are the mind's representations of what we perceive with our senses. They are formed as we experience the world around us, but they may also be summoned up from our memory, or made up from fragments of earlier experience. Usually when we speak of imagery we mean "pictures" in the mind, that is, visual imagery, but we can have images in any of our sensory modes; for example, you will find you can imagine a tune, or the sound of a distant bell (auditory imagery), or a touch, smell, or taste. Anything associated with "imagination" is suspect in our culture, so you may be reassured to know that images are the product of "real" physical events in our brains—nerve cells passing electrical currents and specific

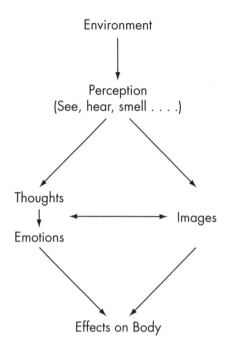

Figure 2.3
The languages of thought and imagery affect the body.

chemicals from one to another. It is also helpful to recognize that imagery is not something exotic. We use it all the time. Imagine, for a moment, that you plan to do some task around the house; if you watch your mind closely, you will detect, flashing through it, a series of images of what you need to do to accomplish the task.

Deliberate use of mental imagery The language of mental imagery has multiple uses, which fall into two broad categories: diagnostic and therapeutic. The former means learning more about what is going on in your mind through examining your imagery. For example, if you imagine and then draw the effect you think your cancer is having on your body, these drawings may tell you quite a lot about your deeper thoughts and fears. You may be able to see something new in them yourself, or you may need the help of a professional to interpret them.

The second broad use of imagery is in trying to make changes in one's mood, or in the body (often both together). For example, relaxation of body and mind may be aided by imagining oneself at the beach. Nausea and pain may sometimes be alleviated by images of peaceful surroundings, or by using symbols; for example, the nausea might be seen as a choppy sea, rendered calm through imagery, or pain seen as a weight, a blade, a fire, being lessened by imagining other symbols that would counteract the pain-inducing ones. Then there are instances where imagery has been used to alter body functions in less obvious ways. For example, scientists researching hypnosis have found, in some people, that certain skin conditions respond to the subject imagining a return to normality; warts, which are tumors caused by a virus, are a case in point. The imagination, primed by suggestion, can do all kinds of things to the body, again in some people more than others. For example, it can cause analgesia (insensitivity to pain) in specific areas, or paralysis of parts of the body, or weals on the skin, even bleeding. In some cultures, anthropologists have noted that when the medicine man puts a hex or curse on a member of the tribe, that person may die suddenly—a dramatic example of the power of mind over body! What these observations tell us is that the mind has potentially considerable powers to influence the body. This does not mean that we can all do these things routinely, but it suggests that there is a great deal of room to learn to use our own minds therapeutically.

Using Imagery as a Way of "Fighting" the Cancer

Plan a regular daily or twice-daily practice of relaxation and imagery. Sitting in a comfortable reclining chair, with your eyes closed, take yourself through a relaxation method, using a tape if it helps. Then bring in the imagery component.

One of our tapes in "Helping Yourself," the workbook and audiotape set put out by the Canadian Cancer Society, contains a combination of relaxation and imagery techniques. The tape asks you to imagine that, with your mind, you can call up a vast army of lymphocytes, the small white cells that help kill many kinds of cancer cells and see them attaching to the cancer cells and destroying them. Then you are to imagine the macrophages, big scavenger cells, coming along after the battle and mopping up the bits of broken-down cell, for recycling. If you are getting chemotherapy or radiation therapy, you can imagine the chemicals or the radiation destroying many cancer cells, and "softening up" others, for easier destruction by the body's defenses. Or you can use more symbolic imagery, visualizing the cancer as, for example, bits of meat, and your defensive system as dogs eating up the meat, or the cancer as small crustaceans and the defenses as fish, swimming around and swallowing them. If you prefer less aggressive imagery, you might instead see your body as a garden and your mind as the gardener, removing the cancerous weeds, and leaving intact the healthy plant cells.

There is no limit to the images you can devise. They need to feel powerful and believable to you, however. So match the defense symbols to the cancer symbols, and make sure the defenses can prevail over their targets. I would suggest doing some reading about imagery as well. Jean Achterberg's books are valuable, as is the Simonton's, and that by Martin Rossman. There are others found in the Reading List at the back of this book.

Imagery is also a powerful way to improve our relations with others. In our classes we do a "resentments" exercise (see Chapter 5), which basically involves imagining a resentful person, looking closely at him or her, and trying to see behind the resentful features and behaviors to the needy individual underneath. We then can imagine surrounding him or her in light, or giving a hug. Similar techniques can be used to strengthen our relationship to religious figures, as we will see in later chapters. We can, for example, imagine talking to or being held by Jesus, Mary, the Buddha, or other figures that have symbolic meaning to us.

* The image that I like to think about is that of me being filled with light. I call this my healing light. My body becomes filled with light and along with the light comes peace, love, happiness, and serenity. But the best part about the light is that it has the ability to melt away the deadly cancer cells, which are excreted through my pores and orifices. I do this imagery lying down with my hands above my head being totally open to the light. I find that when I slowly start bringing the light into my body from the top of my head, it brings a real sense of calmness to me. I think that this imagery also helps me to further relax my body completely.

This chapter has been a brief review of the major self-regulation strategies: learning to relax body and mind, becoming acquainted with the stream of thoughts and beginning to modify them, and starting the process of deliberate use of the language of imagery. The principles themselves are simple enough. Having the self-discipline to practice them and to make changes, is a matter for individual resolve. It may assist your motivation to think of this work as contributing to your personal growth or evolution, over and above any physical healing effect it may have. Nobody wants to be thinking about cancer all the time, as some of our patients put it, so think about it instead as focusing on healing—a much more attractive idea. Once you have worked on these basics for a while, you will be ready to begin the more spiritually oriented work that forms the body of this book. We will meet the basic techniques repeatedly, and in more advanced form, as we pursue our main task of becoming more spiritually connected.

Part Two

The Spiritual Self-Healing Work

3 | Ideas of the Divine and Meditation

We now come to the main focus of the book: working actively to promote our own spiritual connection. The next nine chapters are arranged in a form suitable for a self-study course, working at your own pace. In our classes we do a chapter a week. Each begins with a brief discussion of the central ideas of the chapter, followed by illustrative quotes from written assignments done at home by our patients. Then there are a number of exercises to do—exercises that inspired the responses from patients.

The process of personal spiritual work

It is a challenging process to change old habits of thought and behavior. If you have done psychological work like that described in Chapter 2, you will have learned the truth of this for yourself. The same applies to making spiritual changes. It is easy and pleasant just to read about spirituality, but much more is gained when we become actively involved in doing relevant exercises, like meditation or the introspective projects we describe here. We have also found, from twenty years' experience in helping people in this way, that the impact of the work is greatly enhanced by *writing* about whatever you discover. This crystallizes and concretizes your experiences and insights, and makes them available for future revision and for building upon. These writings can be kept as part of a journal, recording your progress. Don't worry if you are not accustomed to writing: just jot down ideas and findings in point form if you prefer.

At the end of each of the next nine chapters you will find a number of questions to reflect upon, and various exercises to try, notably meditative and imagery techniques. For example, in Chapter 4 we suggest you think about other people whom you resent, listing their "bad" qualities. This is obviously not an academic exercise; the point is to apply it honestly to your own life. Like much of this work, the process can be uncomfortable. In fact, if you don't experience discomfort, you are probably not accessing the relevant thoughts and feelings! Yet even a little progress in such a venture can make a huge difference to your life. In this example, becoming aware of our constant judgmentalism, unwelcome though this insight may be, can lead us to much greater acceptance of others, and hence to more peace and happiness within ourselves and in our relationships. As you reflect on the ideas, let any awareness sink down into your body. You may be able to feel a subtle shift in your physical state as the truth of some new idea becomes evident to you, a kind of "ah-ha" sensation. We have all had such revelations from time to time, as, for example, when we suddenly realize why we acted in a certain way that later seemed out of character.

This work is easier if you belong to a group of fellow students, with a more experienced person as leader if possible, although many people find they can do it alone. If you are a professional conducting a class based on this book, then it is of course important to do the exercises yourself before assigning them to others. To be authentic in this work we must practice what we teach (preach!).

The present chapter invites you to consider what you really think about "God" or the Divine, then introduces meditation. As we have discussed, the basic idea behind connecting spiritually is simple enough. Our true self, it is said, is part of an immortal, self-transcending Divine Mind or God, but this becomes obscured by the "ego" or small self, a collection of impressions and opinions that thinks of itself as separate and all-important. We need to shift focus. (To get an overview of psycho-spiritual healing you can look ahead to Chapter 12, and in particular at Figure 12.1.) When we begin to explore the aspects of ourselves that hinder connection with our deeper spiritual self, the first barrier that we encounter may be doubt, or disbelief, that anything more than ourselves really exists. Sceptics raise arguments like, "If there is a God, why is there evil in the world?"—meaning "Why aren't things the way I would like them to be?" So let's begin by seeing what evidence we can muster that there is a God/transcendent order, or at least that there is more to "reality" than we normally think, leaving room for a divine presence.

Unexamined ideas

Most peoples' ideas about God are hazy, and not examined. Few any longer may imagine an old gentleman with a white beard up in the sky somewhere. But you may think that if God exists, He or She or It is some kind of super-parent, some agent who examines our thoughts and rewards or punishes accordingly. When you look at such beliefs squarely, it appears that they are extensions of our childhood views of our parents, whom we saw as powerful, large figures. You would probably agree that God is not likely to be a material entity, in the sense of being humanoid. When the *Bible* says we are created in God's image, it presumably is referring to mind or spirit within us. Reflect on this question as you do Exercise 1 later in this chapter. It helps to have some clarity about what you think God is *not*, at least. Or you may believe that there is no such thing. If so, ask yourself how you know that. Is the atheistic position any more rational or scientific than theistic beliefs? Or you may return a verdict of "not proven."

Our own experience

This is ultimately the most convincing kind of evidence. The work in this book aims to help you make your own "contact" with a transcendent or divine dimension. As we proceed you may have experiences that can't be rationally explained, e.g., unexpected and highly unlikely events happening to support you, strong feelings of being loved and cared for, even "communications," verbal or intuitive, from unknown sources.

Ideas and evidence about the nature of material reality
Meanwhile (i.e., while waiting for our own experience!), let's examine just how certain our conventional views of reality are. The world is just as we see it, solid, organized into clumps of matter, obeying the laws of thermodynamics. Right? Wrong!

- Modern physics tells us that matter is mostly space. The laws of thermodynamics are not universally valid. Space and time are not absolutes, but depend on conditions of observation. At the atomic level, matter turns out to have various peculiar properties. For example, it is not possible to determine the position and velocity of an electron simultaneously. Changes in a particle can induce similar changes in an associated but distant one at exactly the same time (violating our ideas about cause and effect). The act of observing changes what is observed (as it does also at the psychological level).
- Philosophers East and West have pointed out that what we think we perceive depends on the nature of our sense organs and brains, that is on our biological make-up, on our training, on our current state of mind, and a host of other factors. The view that the world is just as we see it has long been shown to be untenable. Our world is very different from that of a bee or a squirrel. People from different cultures see things differently. An extreme case would be the occasional child raised by wolves or other animals, whose world comes to take on many of the characteristics of the species he or she was nurtured by. Who is to say that "our" current world view is the correct one?
- Although many scientists scoff at the existence of paranormal phenomena, there is now good evidence that the mind can interact with matter in ways that cannot be explained by

conventional science. For example, mental intention alone can influence some physical events (such as the generation of random numbers by machines), and "distant viewing" is possible, namely getting an impression of a distant site that someone else is looking at (these experiments are well documented in *Margins of Reality* by R. Jahn and B. Dunne). There are many reports of out-of-body and near-death experiences. No doubt there can be deception and mistaken interpretations, but I have spoken to a number of sincere people, including people with cancer in our courses, who have had such experiences. My own personal experience includes precognitive episodes, or knowing what would happen in a few minutes to a few hours' time. These can be just as "real" as conventional perceptions, and seem to show that the arrow of time is not inescapably linear and forward moving. In other words, as many have known over the millennia, the world is much stranger than we think, which seems to pave the way for acceptance of realities other than the usual materialistic conception.

- Back in the early 1980s there was a very interesting experiment done, much advertised by New Age writers, in which people who had recently had a heart attack recovered with fewer incidents if they were prayed for by others outside the hospital. The patients did not even know they were being prayed for, and those doing the praying did not personally know the patients and had very few details about them. This experiment has recently been repeated (with a few variations), with a similar result. Both trials were done according to the standards of good technical design. They appear to say that a non-material intervention, prayer, can affect a physical disease (there are also published studies that failed to find such an effect). Other recent studies, for example with people with HIV/AIDS, point in the same direction. And there are even more surprising studies on the effects of "hands-on" healing of people, animals, and plants. A champion of this cause of "non-local" healing is Larry Dossey, a medical doctor who has written a number of good, easily readable books on the subject.

The writings of the mystics

We have readily available to us, in the West, published accounts from all of the great spiritual traditions, from people who have had direct experience of a larger reality or God. The impressive fact is the commonality of experiences related by numerous individuals from widely differing cultures at different points in time. These people are not cranks or simpletons, but are highly intelligent and have often been very influential. The best way to appreciate this is to read, first, an exposition or anthology of spiritual phenomena. A well-known one is Aldous Huxley's *The Perennial Philosophy*. Another, among many, is F.C. Happold's *Mysticism*. Happold writes that mystical experience has manifested itself in similar forms in all parts of the world, giving rise to the expression "the Perennial Philosophy" (a term coined by Spinoza), for which he lists the following common features:

- The world of matter and individual consciousness is only a partial reality and is the manifestation of a Divine Ground or God in which all partial realities have their being.
- Man can know this Divine Ground by direct intuition, which is superior to discursive reasoning.
- Although we are chiefly conscious of the separate ego, we can identify with the spark of our divinity within, that is, with the eternal aspect of ourselves that is part of the Divine Ground.
- It is the chief end of our earthly existence to discover this eternal self.

What our patients have written

* *To me God is not an old gentleman with a white beard up in the sky somewhere. He is not like a parent or powerful figure that makes bad things happen. He has no human characteristics; he is not material, he is not even a "he." I say "he" out of habit. I tried to change what I say to "it" or "she," but I decided that it really does not matter. "He" comes naturally to me when referring to God so "he" it is. In my visualization, I sometimes see a face of a Christ-like being, but I never see a vision of God.*

* *For most of my adult life I've pondered the question over and over of whether or not God exists, and what is the nature of this God. I have hoped for some kind of sign, in a personal experience, that would enable me to know with certainty, that God exists. This need for proof, or at least what my mind considered to be proof, made it difficult for me to accept the idea of a greater spiritual being, in my heart (because I relied on a concrete experiential proof, which didn't appear). I think I have been trying to control how God/Spirit should manifest to me, instead of looking at what already exists in my life and seeing God within that. I've wanted to see a sign so that I can have faith, believing that faith isn't possible without this concrete belief.*

  With the help of the people in my life, the readings I've done, and my own intense motivation, I've started to come out of the box that was holding me back. At some point I started to get a strong feeling of knowing that I had to forget about this idea of finding proof, before committing to belief, and instead to allow myself to feel the faith that I now think exists, in some way, in everyone.

* *I have also felt God around me. . . . He sits now, calmly, quietly and I believe that is God inside of me, and that's the first time I ever thought of God as being a part of me rather than a separate thing.*

* *My views on the possible existence of a higher power are more than a belief system with me—it's a knowing and very difficult to communicate on paper. The feeling of joy that I awaken with each morning; the feeling of being guided even in the most difficult situations—that I am being looked after. When I'm in pain, prayers lessen the pain. I think of God as energy, existing everywhere and in everything, encompassing and enveloping all (sparks of energy) and that each and everyone of us is a spark of that whole. For me that spark can never by extinguished and I have had some of the most beautiful connections with loved ones that have passed from this existence. These experiences I have had are real and, again, have made me feel protected and guided.*

* *I'm taking this course . . . because I have cancer, but the cancer has only been the catalyst. The need existed previously. I am seeking peace in daily living, acceptance in daily living, and a connection to the Divine Power in daily living. If I can find that, then my death and dying, whenever it comes, will be less a cause for anguish, but that will be a by-product, not the goal itself.*

* *What I think God is not is a vengeful and judgmental force ready to punish the individual for his or her sins. The Jewish High Holidays are coming up and that includes Yom Kippur, the Day of Atonement. On this day Jews fast and attend synagogue to pray that their lives will be written in the Book of Life for another year. I remember that as a child I always felt guilty on this day although I never knew what for. As I got older I stopped attending synagogue on that day. I rejected a God who had to be bartered with for another year of life. This was a force to be frightened of, reminding you that you were but a speck of dust, a sinner who had to plead for forgiveness. For many years I held this image of God in my head and abandoned all religious practice. These images represent what God is not.*

* *I "know" a higher power exists. This knowledge is in the core of my being and seems to have always been there. I have never tried to intellectually analyze this feeling as it is beyond words—it seems to me that although the mind is a powerful tool for our use it can be also "the slayer of the Real." I have tried to use my mind and intuition to develop discernment. Of course, another reason that I do not use rational analysis in my definition of the Divine is that my modus operandi is through feeling and experience. I can use the rational mind for doing income tax, balancing my bank account, having some opinions on various and sundry current events, etc., etc., but finding the big picture is beyond my powers of definition!*

Exercises

1. Your views

(a) Write an account of your current views on the possible existence of some higher power, order, intelligence, or God.

(b) What would you regard as evidence? What would it take to convince you?

(c) What kinds of doubts or resistance do you have? Some examples are:

- I haven't seen anything that couldn't be rationally explained.
- I would feel that I was betraying my sense of honesty if I considered something that was beyond my experience.
- I can't turn around now, after many years of not going to church and being an agnostic and say that I hope there is something more.
- Religion is for wimps.

Or perhaps you have had experiences that convinced you of the existence of a higher power. If so, write about them.

2. Your understanding of the Divine

If you believe, or are prepared to consider, that a Divine Power, Order, Intelligence, or Being exists, ask yourself the following:

- What might this be like (assuming for a moment that He/She/It exists)?
- What is God *not* like?
- What is your relationship to this Power? How do you fit into the picture?
- What would convince you of the existence of such a Power?
- What would convince you that it does not exist?

3. Reading

Choose and obtain at least two books written by people who have demonstrated a high degree of spiritual development in their lives and writings. Authors and titles you might consider include:

- *Yoga:* Eknath Easwaran, Paramahansa Yogananda, and Swami Radha; The Bhagavad-Gita
- *Christian mysticism:* John Main, Thomas Merton, Saint Teresa of Avila, and Saint Augustine
- *Buddhism:* Jack Kornfield, Stephen Levine, and Thich Nhat Hanh; The Dhammapada
- *Miscellaneous:* J. Krishnamurti and Eckhart Tolle; *A Course in Miracles*

There are of course many others available. It is important to go to original sources and not be satisfied solely with books by popularizers who write about spirituality, but may not have done a lot of spiritual work themselves. Once you begin reading, write about what you read. It would be most helpful to continue this reading at least for the next several months.

4. Your expectations and goals from this work

(a) What do you expect to "get" from reading this book and doing these exercises?

(b) What are your goals from your spiritual journey? What do you hope to achieve, after working through these chapters, and eventually? (You can revisit these questions after completing Chapter 11 and compare what you experience then from your present experience.)

Mind watching

Mind watching means finding out what you are telling yourself. As was pointed out in Chapter 2, there's a stream of thoughts going through most people's minds almost all the time. Often, much of this thought stream is unrecognized, but it nevertheless controls our moods and behaviors. So one of the very first and most important tasks of self-healing is to get to know what you are thinking.

Sit in a quiet place, and for about ten minutes just observe the thoughts that pass through your mind. Then note down as much of this as you can remember. You won't get it all, but that doesn't matter. The main thing is to start to monitor this flow. This exercise can be done as often as you like, but do it at least three times and write about what you learn.

Meditation

Meditation has been known for thousands of years in many cultures and is now taught widely in the West. While it is often associated with religious faiths, there is no necessary connection. Neither is it related to the occult or the paranormal, although its practice may lead to an expanded view of reality. What is it then? Perhaps the simplest way to describe meditation is to say that it's like listening rather than talking. You could also say that the meditative state is an awareness based on concentration, in the relative absence of thought. Terminology varies, but these definitions express the essence of the process.

Why is it valuable to meditate? You will probably have discovered for yourself how restless the mind is, how it races around from one idea to another. In a sense we are constantly constructing our own little worlds, telling ourselves, for example, that certain experiences are going to be difficult or unpleasant, that someone we know always behaves badly, that we are tired or getting a headache, and so on. We become locked into a few restricted ways of looking at things. Meditation provides us with a simple opportunity to be quiet for a while, and to sense our world and our place in it without these prejudgments. It can thus open doors to radical changes in the thought patterns that create our attitudes. In terms of the "connectedness" discussed earlier, meditation removes some of the blocks put up by the mind that prevent us from fully experiencing the higher, transpersonal levels of ourselves (social, natural world, spiritual). It is like deep relaxation but differs from this or from sleep in that the mind remains alert. In fact, the meditative state of consciousness is different from anything most of us have previously experienced. Good books to read about the subject are Lawrence Leshan's *How to Meditate* and Eknath Easwaran's *Meditation.*

What does it do for health? At the most obvious level, meditation brings relaxation, inducing a state with characteristic brainwave patterns. It has proved useful in diminishing anxiety, addictive behavior, asthma, and hypertension. More generally, it promotes a sense of harmony and interaction that probably reflects an underlying sense of balance in the nervous and hormonal systems. Invoking this balance repeatedly may help to control any disease, including cancer, where regulation is disordered. An Australian psychiatrist, Dr. A. Meares, taught prolonged (two-hour), deep, daily meditation as therapy for cancer patients and reported that of seventy-three people with advanced disease, five showed complete remission, five had marked slowing of the cancer growth, and a much larger portion achieved improved quality of life and significant relief of suffering. This was a clinical study with no control group (i.e., the medical condition of the patients who meditated could not be compared to those of non-meditating patients) but the results are most encouraging.

An exercise in focused meditation There are many methods of meditation. One of the simplest is to use a focus, allowing one thing to take the place of many scattered thoughts. This focus can be an image, one's breathing, a prayer, a series of movements, or a simple word or sound, chanted aloud or repeatedly silently. The work of meditation—and it is work—consists of repeatedly coming back to this focus, pushing other thoughts aside. This has been described as a *passive* effort, an attempt to prevent the usual random thinking.

To begin, sit with the back straight, either on a chair or, if you are supple enough, cross-legged on a thick pillow on the floor. Have the eyes closed, hands resting with palms up on thighs or knees. Drowsiness is more easily avoided if you are not too comfortable. Here are three kinds of focused meditation:

- *Breathing:* Count "one" on the first breath (in and out), "two" on the second breath, etc., up to ten and then start again at one. If your mind strays from the counting, bring it gently but firmly back to the breathing.

- *Word repetition:* This is also known as the Mantra technique. Select a word that has no distracting associations. "Food" would be quite unsuitable! You may wish to try a meaningless word such as "Ah-nam" or one of the words listed below. Repeat your mantra at intervals of a second or two, bringing the mind back whenever your thoughts stray.
- *Imagery technique:* Imagine yourself sitting quietly at the bottom of a clear lake, absolutely still. Every time a thought comes into your head, watch the bubble of air escape and move up to the surface. There are big bubbles for large distractions and small bubbles for minor ones that you nip off before they take your mind away from the exercise.

After a couple of days trying each technique for five minutes or so, select the one you like best, and practice it for fifteen to twenty minutes daily. Most people find the mantra easiest. It can help at first to use a timer, pre-set to give a quiet signal at the end of your meditation.

It is interesting to compare notes with others on your experiences. Did you notice any change in the quality of your mental state as time passed or at the end? Almost all of us, when we begin to meditate, and even after doing it for years, come up against our mind's tendency to wander (if this seems like an insurmountable problem, try the thought-stopping ideas listed in Chapter 5). The patients at our classes are often encouraged (and sometimes diverted) to hear that although I have been meditating daily for over twenty years, I still often have to struggle to quieten my mind!

Selecting a mantra The mantra has been called "protector of the mind," i.e., a focus providing respite from the constant unproductive and often harmful rumination in which we all indulge. Different cultures and traditions have favored different mantras:

- *Christian:* "Lord Jesus Christ have mercy on me" (or just "Jesus" or "Jesu"); "Be still and know that I am God" (or "Be still")

- *Jewish:* "Shalom" (peace); "Echad" (one); Yahweh" (I am)
- *Moslem:* "Allah" (God)
- *Buddhist:* "Buddha"; "Om mani padme hum"
- *Hindu:* "Rama"; "Siva"; "Krishna"; "Om"

These are just a few of many possibilities. Mantras may be longer than this, but they are often simply names for the Divine. They may be a form of prayer. It can be useful to choose a spiritually symbolic word or phrase, one that has been used by many others for centuries, as the words are said to attract an energy or special significance. However, you may also use a neutral sound.

Relationship of meditation to other techniques You may notice great similarities between the state of mind you get into when you do various things, e.g., different kinds of meditation, relaxation, mental imagery, and chanting. Those who practice prayer or contemplation may notice that these also bring about a similar state of consciousness. It is important not to get hung up on what is really meditation and what may be something else. They are all related, all beneficial. The point is to start your own exploration of your inner space, and you will come to know what works best for you. Not everyone can meditate in the way we have described in this chapter. If after a thorough trial you find that it's not for you, return to an approach like deep relaxation or imagery, and don't worry. It is important, however, to practice *some* kind of mental quieting and looking within.

Meditation as an active process In the West we frown upon apparent idleness and habitually pursue various goals with an obsessive, even frantic, busyness. For this reason, many people are initially uncomfortable with meditation, which seems like doing nothing. Yet most of us spend many unproductive hours each week, for example, idly watching TV or surfing the Net. Meditation, despite outward appearances, is an intensely active process that has been likened to the exploration of inner space. It is a route to expand awareness of oneself and one's relationship to the world. The regular withdrawal from others for a time is often rewarded by greatly improving relationships with them during the rest of the day.

Another "hang-up" of our culture is the need to be assured that we are doing things right. The value of meditation lies in the process itself; if you do this, bringing the mind back constantly to a quiet focus, then there is no right or wrong end result, and indeed there should be no particular expectations of outcome. It's worthwhile even if it doesn't seem to go well. Having said this, it must be admitted that there are days when quietening the mind is impossible, often, unfortunately, when we are most distressed. Regular practice will diminish the frequency of these occasions.

Practicing meditation regularly In each of the following four chapters I will describe another kind of meditation, which I strongly suggest you practice daily for twenty to thirty minutes. At the end of this chapter, as well as the next four (which ideally would be spread over five weeks or more), you will be able to pick one approach for continuing practice. If you already have an established practice of meditation, you may want to explore new methods, or you may wish to continue with a method that works for you.

What our patients have written about meditation

* "Om mani padme hum" is the mantra that I use. I like the meaning of "the jewel is in the lotus" or that the Buddha is within us all and that this mantra is used to generate loving kindness and to open one's heart. I have a tape of a chant of this mantra and use that as an aid to meditation. From time to time I also say the mantra during the day while driving the car, walking, doing the dishes, etc., etc. Another favorite of mine is the Jesus prayer "Lord Jesus Christ, Son of God, have mercy on me, a sinner." I feel peaceful and tranquil during meditation and find that the repetition of the mantra helps to calm the endless chatter of the mind.

* *This week has been one of further discovery for me as I find it much easier to go right into my meditation and can actually use the calming impact of the meditation instantly if I need it during my everyday activities. My example of this was when I received my CEA results last week, only to find the levels elevated fifty per cent, which indicates that the cancer has developed a resistance to the chemo we are currently using. My immediate response was that "cold" feeling running throughout my entire body. However, within a matter of a couple of minutes I was totally calm and relaxed and ready to investigate the next step of the medical process. I was able to leave behind the fear and sense of being discouraged and replace it with the calmness.*

Again, a feeling of being full and totally content seems to be the controlling emotion within. Perhaps this is due to the intensity of my meditations and the surrender to the Divine Power just knowing that all will be as it should be and will unfold to me as I need to know.

* *My meditations have undergone some changes. I have begun to wake up at about 4:00 a.m. I decided that since I was awake I'd use this for meditation. As it turns out I've found this to be a great time for me. I seem to be able to still my mind easier and I seem to reach that place of inner peace easier and stay there longer. Also, when I do a healing meditation at this time I experience it differently. It "feels" much more physical in that I actually seem to experience it on a physical level as well as spiritual.*

* *Repeating mantra is taking me deeper into the silence. I experience visions, peace, and harmony. Unaware of time but intuitively know when to come back. Sometimes I drift into the void and cannot recall my experiences. Unaware of the physical. It is as if I am divinely supported in my chair as my mind travels into the velvet blackness of the void.*

4 | Judging

Words can be misleading, so we need to be clear what is meant by "judging" others. Here it refers to any kind of criticism, resenting, blaming, or running down that has an *emotional* charge attached. We are not talking about the kind of dispassionate judgment or discrimination that often has to be made in life, like "She would be better at that job than he would." We are concerned with judgment in the form of resentment—a thought, accompanied by feeling, that so-and-so is not doing what he or she ought to be doing, and usually, is inconveniencing us!

This kind of judgment, to the detriment of others, absolutely permeates the mental life of most people (we will ask you to test this for yourself in the Exercises section). The following is a quote from the written homework of one of our students:

* *When I really scrutinize my reactions to others closely I realize how many thoughts I have that are judgmental of others—often barely noticeable to myself. I have recently been noticing my defensive reactions more, and how defensiveness involves some judgment of the other person (i.e., I am right, so therefore you must be wrong in your*

statements about me . . .). I'm practicing being able to hear critical comments from others as just statements about their thoughts and feelings, without attaching blame (i.e., reacting as if I'm being attacked or blamed, or blaming them in response).

Judgment is perhaps most often of other people, but it is frequently applied to situations also: "The blasted computer is down again!" "This is not part of my job!" Often, when it appears to be directed at a situation, there is a blameworthy person lurking behind it, as in the last example.

What's wrong with this kind of mental behavior? After all, there can be a sense of relief at blaming someone else for discomfort, inconvenience, or threat. And often this seems justified, as when a dangerous driver imperils our safety, or a family member or colleague doesn't seem to pull his or her weight. In this book we are challenging the value, even the validity of reacting to others in a judgmental way, a point of view that cuts across predominant societal custom. Reserve judgment (!) and play along for a while.

The first harmful effect of judging others is that it separates us from them. We feel bad about them, and in return, they usually react negatively to us. "Judge not that ye be not judged," as the *Bible* says.

Second, it is harmful to our own minds and bodies, as well as to our social life. It is worth quoting Easwaran's *Original Goodness* here. If you haven't read any of his books yet, this will give you an idea of his clarity and force:

Indulging in anger (judgment) is pointing a poison-tipped arrow inward, aimed straight at ourselves. It taints our thinking, poisons our feelings, turns our relationships adversarial. If we continue to think resentful thoughts, mistrust spreads in consciousness like some toxic underground chemical until we have a permanent disposition for suspicion. When anger pollutes our internal environment to this extent, we don't need particular events to trigger suspicion; it has become an automatic response, draining us of energy like an insidious hidden leak. Our nervous system and vital organs react angrily on their own, without any connivance from the mind. The long-term effects . . . can be disastrous: heart disease, stroke, extreme emotional stress, perhaps even lower resistance to disease and impaired ability to heal.

As indicated here, anger follows close on the heels of judgment. If we are continually judging that people and things are not as we would like, we will be in a state of chronic anger. (I like Swami Radha's explanation of anger as "frustrated desire.") This wastes our vital energy.

A third effect, the most important, is that judgment separates us from God/the Divine Ground. Why? Because, according to many spiritual systems, we are all a part of God, so if we judge and angrily reject another person, we are rejecting God. This concept will become clearer as you move on with this course.

What our patients have written

* *During the brief period that I was able to devote to this week's exercises I realized that I judge people continually. I have been absolutely unaware or immune to the fact that I am assessing other peoples' worthiness or unworthiness with almost every encounter. It is a habit with no real harm intended but it does cause harm because it separates me from those I judge. I made a long list of things that aggravate me about someone close to me and recognized that it is no wonder that this person feels uncomfortable when we are together. Recognizing this, I intend to make our next visit a lot more comfortable for both of us. I will continue to work at breaking this judging habit and keep a record of the results of my efforts.*

* *I find I have a particularly strong negative reaction to critical/ judgmental behavior in others. When I look at my own behavior I see that I have fleeting judgmental thoughts that I hardly notice at times, e.g., when passing someone I don't know on the street. It used*

to come out more often when I was working and would joke with my colleagues about other people. Sometimes now I notice it after the fact, when I feel a lingering resentment or irritation at someone—I can almost always trace this back to some judgmental thought I've had about them.

* *When I think judgmentally about someone it definitely feels like an attack on them. It is almost like there is this part of me that wants to be mean and wants revenge for the wrong I perceive them as having done to me. It feels like a childish, vengeful part of my personality and it is a struggle to not let it take over; sometimes it wins.*

* *What I have learned:*
  * *Feelings of judgment/criticism and resentment arise when things don't go the way I want them to, which is the frustrated desire Swami Radha was talking about.*
  * *Feelings of resentment often are the result of my feelings of rejection. I realized that I have some deep-seated feelings of rejection from my mother and it clouds my perception of others. I look for rejection. I anticipate it and sometimes I behave in such a manner as to create it (I do this with David [boyfriend]). I have to deal with these issues, or I will continue to feel rejection. But underneath the rejection is frustrated desire [that] someone is not behaving as I would like them to.*
  * *I think my strongest feelings of judgment and criticism are for myself. I judge and criticize myself a lot, which then leads back to the guilt we talked about last week. These feelings hurt me more than anyone else. As long as I am holding on to the feelings, I cannot feel at peace mentally or emotionally, and physically the feelings are putting my body in a state of fight or flight, which will wear it down and prevent it from using its energy to fight my cancer.*

* *I am coming to understand that everything that I do in this life is important and has consequences to the big picture. I feel now (and I didn't before) that smiling instead of frowning or pressing this button rather than that one, or letting someone in front of me in traffic affects the energy in this universe. I never understood that before. I*

didn't think I had any effect on the world. After all, I was no Mother Teresa or Bill Gates. But that doesn't matter. Lots of little ripples can have big effects.

Exercises

1. Our habits of judgment/criticism/resentment

(a) Think of one or more people whom you sometimes resent. List some of the things about them—their behaviors, attitudes, or qualities—that you resent or judge as unworthy, unlikeable, frustrating, or irritating to yourself.

(b) Make a list of all the "hassles" of everyday life that you can think of. How do these inconveniences affect your mental and physical state?

(c) Watch your thoughts as you go about your daily routine. Try to catch yourself "judging," which includes criticizing others, but also the constant process of wanting things to be different from the way they happen to be. List some of these thoughts.

To consolidate what you have learned, it is important to write about it, and to keep this within a journal, which you can add to regularly (a ring binder is convenient). Your notes can be in point form or narrative, handwritten or typed, long or short; but if you don't write them down your insights will often be lost.

2. Competition

(a) Consider how profoundly our Western lifestyle is based on competition—competition for jobs and promotion, for money, in sport, business, the arts, and mass media. In what other areas can you identify it?

(b) Taking sport or games as a prototype:

- What is the effect on you if you compete with someone else and "beat" him or her?
- Is there any suggestion that you are somehow the "better" person for winning?

- How do you feel if you lose? Examine or remember relevant instances and write about their effect on you.

(c) In what areas of your life do you compete?

(d) Do you compete with yourself in any way?

(e) Why do you compete? (Some examples are: for acceptance, recognition, survival, self-glorification, affection, and because everyone does.)

(f) Is there any need to compete/achieve on the spiritual path? Why or why not?

(g) How is this topic related to judgment of others (and of oneself)?

3. Cancer as "opportunity"

It is sometimes said that problems, even severe challenges like cancer, are "gifts," "lessons," or "opportunities." (For example, the I Ching defines crisis as "danger plus opportunity.") What is your reaction to that? Do you see potential benefits in your cancer or other life crises, mixed in with the pain? Are there examples (of which this may be one) in your life where an initial entirely negative judgment gives way to an assessment that a situation contains both unwanted and beneficial aspects?

Mind watching

This exercise, as described in Chapter 3, should be repeated until you form the habit of continuously monitoring your stream of thoughts.

Sitting and watching the mind, coupled with trying to keep it still, or at least not allowing a train of associations to develop from any thought, is itself a form of meditation or mindfulness. The hope is to transfer this mindful state to our daily activities, so that we "just do things" without the constant round of vague resentments, regrets, and irritations that normally accompanies many of them (you will need to check this out for yourself). A modern author who has written a truly excellent book about this is Eckhart Tolle (*The Power of Now*). As he points out, by keeping the mind focused and relatively still we remain "in the present moment" or "in the now." Again, confirm for yourself that much of the time we are ruminating about past events (usually with regrets of various kinds) or anticipated future events (with attendant anxiety), rather than being firmly in the present moment.

Journaling

To reiterate, what happens in our minds can affect the progress of physical disease. We try to change mental attitudes using relaxation and meditation to drop stressful thoughts, and using imagery, to insert positive "blueprints" for change. We also try to become increasingly more aware of what thoughts and feelings pass through our minds, in order to be able to choose whether to retain them or not. An important technique for improving this awareness is keeping a daily journal of significant events.

The process is quite simple. At the end of the day (or at some other regular time), review the things that have happened and write a brief account of the main things that had an impact on you—these will often be interactions with others. In particular, record events that aroused emotions in you—anger, joy, fear, sadness, irritation, etc. Try to re-create the scene in your mind and uncover what you were telling yourself that induced the emotional reaction. Can you think of alternative ways of thinking or behaving that, in retrospect, would have been healthier?

Meditation and journal keeping complement each other. The meditation gives you more access to formerly unconscious reactions, and the journaling clarifies and captures these, promoting an awareness that permits change. We can also use a journal for catharsis—pouring out bottled-up emotions in a safe way. We can write letters (not for sending) to people we have resented. We can include drawings, plans, notes from lectures or books, press clippings (especially of positive events), and records of dreams. You will need a special notebook: a ring binder is convenient, as you can then file various papers in it. It is helpful to review the contents and make a summary each month. Sometimes, if you are living with others, there is concern about ensuring privacy for the frank descriptions of one's actions and thoughts. Indeed, if this does not cause concern it may be that you are not expressing things that are important. The journal can be locked away, or you can use a code for sensitive disclosures. Also, put a note on the cover requesting that others do not read the contents.

Reliving a recent event Here is a useful exercise to provide material for your journal. After a brief relaxation, bring to mind an event from the last day or days that generated an emotional reaction in you. Try to relive it in your imagination: it will be like rerunning a movie, or video, which you can stop and start at will. What thoughts were going through your mind? What feelings did you experience? Did the situation or people involved remind you of any previous events?

After these explorations, *write down* what you have learned. Doing so is much more valuable than simply musing. Were you able to "observe" yourself, from the outside, as it were, interacting with others in your daily activities? Could you capture thoughts and feelings associated with the events you remembered? This detached observation of yourself becomes easier with practice— you'll soon find yourself doing it during the events themselves— and it is an indispensable preliminary to changing habits. Without self-observation and self-awareness we are like sleepwalkers, caught up in our habits without realizing what we are doing.

Self-awareness: Watching your mental and physical habits You can extend this exercise of watching yourself to all aspects of your life, whether stressful or not, and be pleasantly surprised at what you will learn. Try to identify feelings associated with events, as they are much more important than intellectual ideas. For example, you might be interested in watching yourself as you meet and talk to people. Ask yourself, "Do I feel nervous? Is my body reacting? Can I remember names, and if not, why not? Am I worrying about what he or she thinks of me?" After a while, this is like having a benevolent inner observer or witness of your thoughts and actions.

Meditation

For this week the technique is "Hamsa—Soham." This is a mantra used in synchrony with the breath. "Soham" means "I am He," and "Saham" means "I am She." In using this mantra we are asserting our identity as part of God or the Divine Ground. Another translation I have seen is: "I am That; That I am."

As you breathe in (through the nose if possible), silently repeat "Ham"; as you breath out repeat "So" or "Sa." Alternatively, you can say "Hamsa" as you breathe in, and "Soham" as you breathe out (I like this better myself). Bear in mind the sense of the mantra as you repeat it, but as in all meditation, don't allow the mind to "run away" with it, to editorialize, analyze, or "embroider."

5 | Forgiveness

Forgiving others is almost universally recognized as a noble human capacity. Here are some excerpts from the writings of Paramahansa Yogananda, in his commentary on a major Indian spiritual text, the *Bhagavad Gita* ("God Talks with Arjuna"):

> Forgiveness in the man of God consists of not inflicting, or wishing to inflict, punishment on those who harm or wrong him. He knows the cosmic law will see to it that all injustices are rectified; it is unnecessary and presumptuous to attempt to hasten its workings or to determine their form. . . . This is not to say that wrongdoers should have no curtailment . . . (but) those whose duty it is to enforce just laws . . . should mete out (justice) without malice or a spirit of revenge.

He goes on to say that "one should forgive under any injury," a quote from another Indian text (the *Mahabharata*) that reminds us of the biblical injunction to "turn the other cheek."

Dr. Gerald Jampolsky, in his book *Goodbye to Guilt*, probes even deeper. He points out that forgiveness, as it's usually understood, often has overtones of condescension, or even of repressed aggression:

> *The ego would have us practice "pseudo-forgiveness." In effect it says: "I can forgive you because I am superior to you. Therefore I will sit on my anger and repress it, rather than be consciously aware of my desire to kill you, which is what you really deserve." This pseudo-forgiveness only reinforces guilt, because it is a double message that continues to emphasise the unhealed separation between the "innocent" and the "guilty."*

What, then, is true forgiveness? The conventional view is that when we forgive, we first make a judgment of another, then are sufficiently magnanimous to overlook their "sins"! In fact, true forgiveness means recognizing that the problem is within ourselves. It arises from our willingness, even eagerness, to judge, and to claim that the source of all our problems lies outside of ourselves, usually at the feet of someone else. Our aim must be to identify this tendency, and cut it off at the root, so to speak; that is, to recognize when we are judging and try to stop doing so.

Choosing only love

Learning to drop such emotionally charged, self-serving judgment is the central task of the spiritual journey. You may not believe this at first—you may not be aware of how prevalent your judging is. Remember, the first requirement for progress in this kind of work is not to reject automatically anything we don't immediately see. Keep an open mind, in other words, and test out the idea in your own life. The first step is to learn to recognize what we are doing. As we identify our judgmental thoughts we will try to replace them with thoughts of forgiveness, affection, and tolerance. You can use the mantra "choose only love" to help with this. "Love" in this sense is not the romantic love of worldly affairs, but a sense of caring, compassion, and connection that asks nothing of the object of our concern (discussed further in Chapter 8).

What are the spiritual effects of forgiving others, and ultimately ourselves? It allows us to experience love, for others, for ourselves, and for the Divine. We cannot really love while we are blaming. Even a small amount of progress will leave space for unconditional love that may never have been there before. The *Bible* puts it the other way: "Perfect love casteth out fear," but from the point of view of the struggling seeker, it is the practical work of "casting out fear," anger, and judgment that is needed to enjoy perfect love. To achieve this is to remove the separation from God. Gerald Jampolsky expresses it this way:

> The healed mind does not know the meaning of separateness. Because it contains only God's loving thoughts; it is peaceful and devoid of guilt, pain, and conflict. Its identity is its perfect harmony with the wholeness of love.

What our patients have written

* When I see people with love, I think they are more likely to see me with love also. My loving channel is definitely open for business. I've really noticed a difference in my life. People seem to like me more, want to be with me. It feels good, it feels right, it's tough work, but mostly, it's so liberating, because I'm not wasting all my energy passing judgment on things, formulating opinions and trying to get others to agree with my opinions. I am still touched by negative emotions (hard habit to break), mainly because in my past I have been very jealous of other people. Jealousy is not a good channel. It's really exhausting!

* A person in my family causes problems for me by making it difficult to see my son and grandchildren. She tried different things such as pretending to be sick, or piling up tasks that could have been done earlier and creating chaos.

   I chose to see this person only with love. I see now that she is a person who fears that there is only a limited amount of love for her available coming from my son. And she needs it for herself.

   I am now able to separate her actions from her as a person. I choose only love and I do not feel angry and resentful any more. I also do *not make any demands on my son or on her. This leaves the other person free to seek contact when they are ready.*

* *Recently a bank teller worked at a snail's pace. I had to wait a long time before my turn came. I was irritated and about to say something when I remembered "choose only love." I could see she was nervous and scared. So I asked if she was new at the branch and smiled. She said yes, and everything proceeded better. So I opened a good channel in myself.*

* *I only wish it were as easy to love everybody else as if they were our children. Gradually I start to see that love is the key to forgiveness. I usually felt that forgiving somebody who hurt me meant that what they did was okay, and that stopped me from forgiving them. Now I am starting to realize that if they were my children, although I may not approve of what they did, I could still love and forgive them.*

* *When feeling centered, I project feelings of love, appreciation, approval, and acceptance. In taking ownership of my feelings I move out of blame and shame and find less resentment within my relationships. In reviewing my memories of past confrontations, I became aware of how I was being affected by the unwillingness to let go of the emotions of these issues. This understanding of myself helps me to acknowledge the innocence in each of us. We are doing the best we can and as we open to our higher selves we will do better. Viewing difficult people as innocent children helps me to center myself and look beyond the behavior and stimulates my proactive response in a loving way. . . .*

When I open the love channel in my relationships there is less competition and more sharing involved in the interaction. I am more aware of their need to talk and me to listen without jumping ahead and mentally forming a response. In this channel I am able to deflect the negative emotions because I recognize they do not belong to me.

Exercises

1. Separating a person from his or her behavior

Taking an individual from the exercise in the last chapter, or some other whom you resent and have personal contact with, try considering the essence of the person as separate from his or her behavior. Think about that person, then think about what he or she does that has annoyed you as if that person were a small child, or a robot, and had no control over his or her actions. Does this make a difference in how you view him or her?

2. Replaying an emotional incident

Recall a recent instance where someone criticized, made demands upon, or otherwise inconvenienced you. It need not be a dramatic example and might best be a situation with someone you know well.

Now "play through" the incident in your mind, as if through a videotape. Note carefully what you thought and felt at each point, in particular, your reactions to the alleged injustice of it. Then go through it again, but this time, before you begin, fill yourself with light, as in the "Divine Light" exercise below. Repeat to yourself, "I choose to see this person only with love," or some similar affirmation. Holding on to this feeling, let the other do his or her thing (in your mind), and note any changes in your reaction.

You could do this a number of times, with different examples, in your imagination. As the opportunities arise, try it out in real life.

3. Using the "love channel"

Interacting with other people is a complex business. As we all know, there is a lot going on during the conversation. We can think of having a number of "channels" connecting us with the other—a judging channel, an angry one, a controlling one, a delighted, pleased, and loving one, and so on. We can choose which of these channels we keep open or shut. So when you are talking to someone, try consciously to think of just holding the "loving channel" open. Note how this feels. Since there is only this "good" channel available, can the other person touch you with any negative emotions?

Mind watching and thought stopping

Please don't neglect the basic process of learning to watch the mind. Repeat it until you have constant, ready access to your stream of thoughts.

If the mind won't be still, either while trying to meditate or at times of anxiety (for many, that period of lying awake worrying in the early hours of the morning), there are a number of things you can try:

- Write down your problems to take them off your mind.
- Practice relaxation before meditating.
- Experiment with different times of the day for your meditations. It may prove easier to concentrate early in the morning.
- Set yourself a "worry period" when you are allowed to worry as much as you want, for example, between 8:00 and 8:15 a.m. each day. Then whenever you find anxious thoughts surfacing, tell yourself that you will deal with them during your worry time. Alternatively you can set a timer for a few minutes, allow yourself to ruminate until it rings, then snap your fingers, shout "Stop" and do so!
- Try a "worry fast." This is a related technique where you set, in advance, a day when you will not allow worries.

Meditation

The Divine Light Mantra This mantra meditation comes through the late Swami Sivananda Radha, with whom my wife and I had the great good fortune to study at intervals over many years. The first four lines are a traditional mantra; the last was added by Swami Radha. The invocation is recited, silently or aloud, while invoking or imagining light streaming down from above, flowing into the body through the head, and filling the entire being.

I am created by Divine Light
I am sustained by Divine Light
I am protected by Divine Light

I am surrounded by Divine Light
I am ever growing into Divine Light.

The full practice has been described by Swami Radha in a booklet called *The Divine Light Invocation,* or alternatively in her monumental work on spiritual development, *Kundalini Yoga for the West.* The following is an adaptation.

Sit or stand with your eyes closed. Relax and repeat the mantra twice slowly, the first time through trying to see light filling you, and the second time feeling it. Think to yourself that every cell of your body, every level of consciousness, is filled with light, and see yourself as well, healthy, and whole. Then share this light by imagining someone in need standing before you and receiving light that you send from the area of your heart. See this person filled with light also. If you prefer, you could substitute "the love of God" for "Divine Light," although it helps most people to visualize light, whatever the affirmation they are using.

Try this practice daily, thinking of it as a means of forgiving others, and yourself.

Additional meditation An extremely useful and relatively simple way of meditating is to chant aloud, using a simple prayer or mantra as the text. This method is commonly used in various spiritual traditions, including Hinduism, Buddhism, and Christianity. An advantage of expressing the sound audibly compared with just thinking it is that it seems to dissipate some of the restlessness that we often experience in attempting to meditate—it gives the body something to do, as it were.

There are a number of tapes and books of chants on the market. If possible, accompany yourself on an instrument, or have a tape playing along with you. Three tapes that we use in our classes are put out by the Wings of Song group: "Sri Ram, Jai Ram" (Hail to the Lord, in the form of Rama), "Om Nama Siva" (honoring another form of the deity, Siva), and "Gloria" (from the Christian Catholic tradition). Note that chants should be very simple and repetitive; the mind should not be distracted by trying to remember what to do next. The simplest method of all is to chant "Om" in a mono-tone. This is said by some to be the "root syllable of the Universe." It has certainly been used for chanting by millions of people over millennia. Inhale through your nose if possible. Try chanting for about twenty minutes daily for a while and, as always, write about your experiences.

> * *The greatest influence I have on my moods is meditation. When I can concentrate and meditate, I have found that I can still everything and concentrate on reaching another level of awareness. Lately, combining together the lessons in the* Course in Miracles *and the* Qi Gong *physical exercises I am learning has been the most effective way of sealing ideals into my body—a rather odd concept that works with me. I used to depend on smells to bring back memories; now I realize that rhythmic chanting and rhythmic movements can help set ideas in my mind (now that I think about it, something that has probably been around in all religions for thousands of years). As usual I have to discover it myself before recognizing its universality, and realizing why it is so effective.*

6 Guilt, Self-Criticism, and Self-Acceptance

One way of describing the spiritual journey is to say that it is a quest for one's true nature or identity. We almost always have a false idea of who we are, and the most harmful of our views are the judgments and criticisms that we make of ourselves. This self-condemnation makes us feel guilty and inadequate. It often engenders a deep sense of shame and personal unworthiness. We may not immediately recognize this: "Who, me? I'm not guilty of anything. I'm quite content with myself, thanks very much." This sort of obliviousness to what is going on in the deeper reaches of the mind is caused, as Freud pointed out, by the "layers" of defensiveness that we construct, to conceal from ourselves our true thoughts and feelings. We need first of all to find or identify these suppressed ideas, bring them out into the open, as it were, after which we will have the choice, previously unavailable, to let them go.

"Guilt" is one of those words, like "love" or "God," that has multiple meanings and signifies different things to different people. Conventional psychology has a fairly narrow definition—essentially the regret and self-criticism we feel about actions in the past. Christian theology adds other elements that can be confusing, for example, the idea of "sin," those actions of which it is assumed a deity would not approve. For the kind of psycho-spiritual work we are engaged in here, we want to understand how we regard ourselves at the deepest possible level, then examine this self-image and see how much of it is true and what effect it has on our relationship to the Divine. So I will adopt the very broad definition used by Ken Wapnick, perhaps the foremost interpreter of *A Course in Miracles* (ACIM):

> Guilt is really the sum total of all the negative feelings, beliefs, and experiences that we have ever had about ourselves. So guilt can be any form of self-hatred or self-rejection; feelings of incompetence, failure, emptiness, or feelings that there are things in us that are lacking, missing or incomplete.

Where do these self-judgmental attitudes come from? It may seem that the only significant criticisms arrive from outside, from other people, whereas in fact the important critical voices are internal. Often they echo old voices from the past: the remarks of parents, teachers, family, or peers that have settled firmly in our minds, and influenced our own reflections on our self-worth. This may cause a distorted, usually poor, self-concept that limits us greatly. Conventional psychology recognizes this, and strives to help people reclaim a better opinion of themselves. In spiritual psychology we want to begin with a healthy self-respect and then go far beyond this to an understanding of our true nature, which is, as the mystics of all traditions tell us, that we are each part of a larger Order, Intelligence, or Mind. Our sense of guilt keeps us from knowing this oneness with the Divine. *A Course in Miracles* puts this very directly, as Wapnick points out:

> The ultimate source of all [our] guilt is the belief that we have sinned against God by separating ourselves from Him. As a result of that, then, we see ourselves as separate from everybody else and from our [Higher] Self."

A further consequence of feeling guilty, whether or not we realize it consciously, is that we expect punishment, which generates fear. We feel that we must do something to ward off this punishment. For this purpose we use various strategies, one of which is suppressing or repressing (a deeper burying of the ideas than suppressing) our guilt and fear. Two other strategies are to "attack" or "punish" ourselves (in a kind of "pre-emptive strike" aimed at deflecting outside intervention) and to "project" our guilt on to others, that is, attribute our motives to other people (a mechanism we will examine further in the next chapter). Dr. Gerald Jampolsky points out some of these consequences of feeling guilty in his book *Goodbye to Guilt*:

> It is a psychological fact that if we hold on to guilt, we will attempt to handle it either by attacking ourselves (frequently expressed as symptoms of depression or physical illness), or projecting the guilt on to someone else.

In other words, as well as keeping us separate from the Divine, our self-condemnation may cause illness, fear, and problems with our relationships. We seem to have parachuted directly into what may be a fundamental cause of our problems! Our work now is to try to identify self-criticism or condemnation in ourselves so that we will be able to counter it, because it is unfortunately true that these ways of defending ourselves against buried guilt, while bringing short-term comfort, greatly distort our view of ourselves and our relationship to our world.

What our patients have written

* Recognizing that the reason I feel rejection by others so painfully is that it mirrors the rejection that I have done to myself is definitely a new way of looking at myself and at others. I guess it is one small step towards self-knowledge. How can I honestly harbor ill feelings towards the people who have rejected me, when their rejection of me is

so much less than my rejection of myself? The problem isn't with them, it is with how I have treated myself. The solution isn't going to come through others, I have to learn to love myself.

* *With the beautiful quote from Diane Berke's book* The Gentle Smile *in mind, I broke my life down into various time frames and for each period listed all my feelings of inadequacy and all actions or thoughts which cause me to feel guilt. My list is four pages long, single-spaced. I'm not sure whether I'm being too hard on myself or just too thorough but I felt a real need to devote a lot of energy and honesty to this exercise. I hadn't thought of many of the things on my list for years. Some made me cry and all made me aware that I have used every strategy mentioned in the notes to deal with my guilt and fear of punishment. As I reflected on my list I realized that I have been taught that these failings are sins against God and that they keep me from being close to Him. Forgiveness through self-forgiveness is new to me and because I have used all means to push my sins or errors away from my consciousness I have never felt the peace of forgiveness. I have experienced sadness, sorrow, avoidance, denial, and depression at various times in my life over some of the things on my list. An example, my mother's sudden death left me in shock. I felt guilty about not having been supportive enough as she coped with life's problems. And I couldn't do anything about it after she died. I'm certain that it was guilt that caused a reactive depression.*

* *I surrounded myself with God's light and knowing that he has forgiven me and that I am part of God, I reviewed my long list of errors. Some of them made me feel very sad and brought me to tears again, but I continued to focus on "choose only love." It is healing. I felt a sense of relief and even joy at having confronted these issues that have kept me from forgiving myself and others. Self-forgiveness reminds me that the past is gone and that I am free to choose love today. I believe that for me, true and lasting forgiveness will take time. I will continue to practice self-forgiveness.*

* *In looking over the lists I realize that the guilt-inducing words, thoughts, and deeds came from my lack of self-knowledge, mindful-*

ness, and clarity. The motivations were fear, ignorance, desire, lack of love, etc.—those feelings we are trying to understand in the healing journey—rather than a conscious desire to harm. Even though I have forgiven myself because I know that I acted in those moments with all that I was at that moment, I still remember the physical pain of suffering guilt. I try to look at those events in my life with compassion, understanding, and forgiveness.

* *I honestly have trouble "feeling a light" and self-forgiveness (and forgive me, again, I feel guilty about this too!) . . . Alas, I only shift to new sources of guilt. What I have been able to realize is that in the grand scheme of things, my guilt is almost laughable . . . how trivial, really . . . but I still recognize that it is mine, I own it, it influences just about everything I do, and it runs very deep within me! Perhaps I need more than one week on this chapter! (I am chuckling now at this understatement.)*

  I am also chipping away at my inclination to seek constant improvement and perfection and vacillate between feeling anxious at "easing up" and more peaceful at being able to let go of some of my deeply ingrained habits. "That's good enough" is a phrase that makes me shudder in dismay and wrestle with my conscience, but perhaps it will help me heal my life!

* *I was finding it difficult to let go the long habit of not forgiving. It was an almost comforting rut; however, along with the harsh judgment of others were equally harsh judgments of myself. As I began to understand this, I was able to see myself as the small child that needed as much compassion as those whom I could not forgive.*

Exercises

As Diane Berke says in *The Gentle Smile*, "the healing process is one of bringing the darkness in our minds to the gentle light of awareness." So approach this process of digging up the self-critical voices in a spirit of compassion for yourself—much as if you were trying to find and remove a number of painful thorns.

1. Investigating guilt

(a) List any areas of your life in which you feel, or have felt, inadequate or incompetent, or where you have felt like a failure or incomplete in some way.

(b) Likewise, list anything you do, or can remember having done, about which you experience guilt, self-condemnation, self-hatred, or judgment. (If you are sharing your ideas with others you may need to use a code to list some of these things, and/or to keep part of it private.)

(c) Can you sense this guilt as an "attack" on yourself? What does it feel like in your body?

The above lists should occupy at least a page, and probably more. When I did the exercise I found it helpful to break my life up into sections ("early school," "high school," "early married life," etc.), and list the self-criticisms dominant at each time. To counter any feelings of frustration or depression the exercise may have left you with, do the following:

• Look at the list, reading through slowly, and tell yourself that this is all in the past; that these things all had a reason, they were errors and peculiarities for which you now forgive yourself completely, and that they are already forgiven by the Divine. Affirm that, in thinking about yourself and your past, you will "choose only love." See yourself surrounded by light as you do this. Imagine this light as God's presence all around and within you.

• If you like, make a copy of the list that you can burn while practicing self-forgiveness. Write about any shift in feelings that may have accompanied this.

2. Forgiveness of oneself

(a) See yourself in light. Then see a religious figure, like Jesus, the Buddha, Divine Mother, or your Inner Healer (more on this below) embracing you. Imagine as you do this that you are giving up the habit of constantly wanting things to be different.

(b) Once you have done this, write down answers to the following:

- How do you feel about yourself now? Has the judgment and guilt abated? Is it easier to accept yourself?
- Is this a passive (apathetic) process (i.e., giving up), or an active one, requiring effort?
- Does it bring peace of mind?

3. The Inner Healer

There is a great deal of evidence that the deeper or unconscious mind has both a detailed "knowledge" or record of events in the body and great potential ability to control them. For example, with a biofeedback apparatus, people can learn to control their blood pressure, heart rate, brainwave patterns, smooth muscle contractions, and even the firing of certain single nerve cells. Placebo (inert) medications, or suggestions under hypnosis, can lead to cures or healing changes in a variety of conditions, e.g., peptic ulcer, pain, various skin diseases, asthma, and arthritis. We attempt to use some of this potential control in our exercises with imagery. One way of contacting this inner wisdom is to imagine a figure or "healer" within, who may not only embody the potential of our deeper minds, but also serve as a route to contact our spiritual dimension.

Inner Healer exercise

First relax deeply, and then imagine yourself on a path leading into the woods. There, as you wait in a clearing, imagine you are approached by an animal "guide." Talk to this animal, noticing your feelings toward it. The guide can then lead you deeper into the forest to a second clearing, in which there is a dwelling of some kind, inhabited by the Inner Healer. Knock on the door and wait for the Inner Healer to come out. This may be a wise old person, a religious figure, somebody from your past, another animal, a ball of light, a voice without a body, or one of many other symbols. You can have a dialogue with this figure, asking for information and help, and responding with gratitude. At the end of the conversation, have the original guide take you back to the first clearing, from which you can return to your normal "reality."

The experience of an Inner Healer Some people immediately get powerful images and "messages" from an Inner Healer; others experience very little at first. You may simply get a sense of "presence," without images—that's fine. If not much is happening for you, it is likely that you are blocking the experience with scepticism or pre-judgments as to what should happen. We know that there is a great deal of unconscious wisdom in everyone, expressed, for example, in dreams. So don't despair if nothing happens on the first few attempts, but continue to work away at the process patiently.

A concern expressed by many of our patients is that they are "just making it all up." This need not be a problem. Where imagery is sluggish, it is legitimate to help it along with conscious thought. The real measure of usefulness in all of the Inner Healer work is how unexpected or novel the messages are. If you already consciously know all that you are experiencing, then there has been no learning. If you have had new insights and experiences, it doesn't much matter how you arrived at them. We do the work to uncover hidden potential.

Sometimes frightening images come up. If you are working alone, you may prefer to drop them and come back to concentrating on your breathing. If you wish to confront and master these images or thoughts, which is therapeutically valuable, this is best done with the help of an accredited psychotherapist.

*   *Whenever I imagine myself struggling against this disease, I am joined and comforted by my Inner Healer. He is a Jesus-like figure. I am able to gain immediate comfort whenever I feel the need to "summon" my Inner Healer since this image comes to me at some level very easily.*

    Cancer appears to me as spots with a black core, surrounded by purple, surrounded by yellow. My Inner Healer brings light to my body and when I feel completely filled with light, I see the cells or spots gradually melt away. I believe that I can co-exist with this disease. I am comforted that my Inner Healer will always be with me, sending in light and melting away cancer cells as they grow.

Meditation

The technique to try for this week is "mindfulness." It is commonly associated with Buddhism, but is used in many spiritual traditions. The process can be very like the mind watching you have been doing, i.e., simply noticing thoughts as they pass through, but not following them up in any way. If you find that a sensation, sound, or idea comes to your attention, just "watch" it and let it go. A device that helps you keep on track is to repeat over and over to yourself a word or phrase describing what you are currently focusing on, e.g., "back pain, back pain" or "when can I stop, when can I stop," until the mind shifts to something else. You can think of this process as slowing down the mental videotape.

For background reading, try any of the books by Thich Nhat Hanh, such as *The Miracle of Mindfulness*, or read one of the books by Jon Kabat-Zinn or Eckhart Tolle mentioned in the Reading List.

* *In general I found "mindfulness meditation" easier to do than other forms that I have tried. A thought would come into my mind and I would choose one word to describe it and say it over and over. Sometimes I said it only three or four times before another thought came into play, and other times I would say it ten or more times before I would think of something else. I found that I would say the word over in my mind quickly at first but as the thoughts came and went I was gradually thinking the word to describe the thought much more slowly, as if the act of meditating was slowing my thinking process down as I got more into it.*

7 | Judging as a Projection of Our Guilt and Frustration

Now we come to a function of the mind that is rather tricky, but very important. We have a number of ways of avoiding unpleasant ideas and emotions. Freud called these "defenses." One we will readily recognize is "denial"—refusing to look at or acknowledge what is actually taking place. A second is "projection"—which is the shifting of blame and responsibility to someone else for qualities or ideas that really arise within ourselves. For example, if I have the desire to control someone else's behavior, I may reject this possibility in myself and instead attribute controlling desires to others. This shift typically takes place without our being aware of it. Or I may feel very angry, but as I am unwilling to let myself feel this, I'll point to angry behavior in others. In a slightly wider sense, if I feel angry or frustrated about something that is making me unhappy, I may blame others for it, rather than myself. So if I am suffering from a diagnosis of cancer, I may look around for someone or something that I can hold responsible for my distress: doctors, the health-care system, God, anyone. It is a kind of unloading of the responsibility for misery and guilt. The real problem is my self-talk and my fears about what may happen, but instead of looking at this I lash out at the external situation. Projection is a spinoff from self-criticism. You can check this out for yourself by imagining (in a relaxed state) that you are absolutely free of any self-criticism; then you would not blame anyone else for anything (see Exercise 2, below).

Ken Wapnick, in *Talk Given on a Course in Miracles*, has an excellent metaphor for understanding projection. He suggests we think of projection as a movie projector. Imagine that you are the movie projector and that you have your own film of guilt (self-criticism) that you are always playing through. You project the guilt from this film onto the screens of these people and then see your own negative thoughts about yourself as coming from them. The ego, or separate self, reasons this is the way to get rid of one's guilt—it is too devastating a thought to deal with otherwise.

This can be a difficult concept to grasp at first, so let's have another look at it, and relate it to what we have done in the earlier chapters. We like to think that all of our problems and distress are caused by agents or situations outside ourselves. The psychoanalyst Karen Horney called this process "externalization." We do it to feel more comfortable in the short term. It is a blanket term, within which we can put several common types of perception:

- "Judgment" means that we consider a person/thing/situation is not as it should be (remember, we are concerned here with the kind of judgment that has an emotional charge to it, not with dispassionate discrimination).
- "Blame" is similar to emotionally charged judgment, but here we are usually emphasizing the unpleasant effect someone or something is having on ourselves.
- "Projection" is the term from Freud, meaning essentially that we blame others for our problems, but don't know we are doing it (i.e., it's an unconscious "defense" mechanism). It includes the action of criticizing in others the qualities that we unknowingly deplore in ourselves.

Why do we use these distorted ways of thinking? Basically, to avoid looking into ourselves, to remove the apparent responsibility for our distress away from ourselves and from our guilty deeper knowledge that it is *we* who are causing this distress (by our reaction to events, and our self-talk). *Talk Given on a Course in Miracles* probes this process to its depths, pointing out that the ultimate cause of our guilt—of all negative self-appraisal—is our separation from the Divine, or God. We feel alienated, vulnerable, and at some level we know we have done this to ourselves. So we lash out at others.

What is needed? All of the great wisdom traditions tell us that we need to take responsibility for our own thought processes. This means honestly looking at all of our opinions and judgments. Does this mean we are responsible for our illnesses? No (at least not the levels of awareness that most of us have), but we are, as Stephen Levine, author of *Who Dies*, puts it, responsible *to* our illnesses, that is, to do all we can to understand and help ourselves, using illness as a motivator. More generally, we are responsible for using this life as a way of learning who we really are.

Projection is one of the ways in which we create our own worlds, our own reality. An important part of the early work in spiritual growth is coming to understand this, and consequently accepting responsibility for our personal world. On encountering this idea for the first time a common reaction is, "I didn't cause those earthquakes/wars/examples of poverty and injustice, my cancer, etc." My suggestion would be not to turn to major and apocalyptic world events in your haste to deny this possibility. After all, if it has any validity, it might provide you with a handle on your world. For the present, test it out on relatively small-scale events in your own surroundings. In particular, look for evidence that, by your mental actions and attitudes, you are creating conflict between yourself and other people, because if we judge others, they know it and will react in kind.

What our patients have written

   * *Indeed, this has been a difficult concept to grasp. It helped me to first look back at some of the people in my life that I have blamed for past and present events and situations. I analyzed a few of them carefully*

and in each case I found that I was judging another because of the guilt I was experiencing at having done or not done something.

* *Our neighbor is a very inquisitive person. She is very direct and asks for information with no hesitation whatsoever. She needs to know what goes on in people's lives. Upon reflection I am also inquisitive but I try to get information indirectly. I am guilty of the same habit. I tell our friends about the "busy lady" next door. I now see that I am projecting my guilt to her—I need to change my attitude.*

* *When I feel sorry for myself because my spouse isn't paying attention to my fears and frustrations, I really am projecting my own sense of guilt at not being as attentive to her as I should be. This is very often at the root of our disagreements. Very recently I have made a deliberate effort to check this reaction. Arguments and bad feelings that have been often associated with these disagreements do not occur, which seems to confirm the existence of my projection problem. It's also interesting that in managing the reactions, not only is the inter- action calmer and positive, the result is I feel more reasonable, more responsible and a lot less guilt.*

* *In the process of watching my thoughts for judgments, it has become clear to me that my judging activity is often directly related to my state of mind at the time. The judgments, in fact, appear to be a reflection of my own state (more often than not) rather than an actual assess- ment of what others are doing and saying. The classic "People are just getting in my way," or "They're too slow," or even the fairly benign "Where have they all come from?" is just a reflection of the fact that I may simply have not left sufficient time for myself to get some- where, and I cover my own guilt feelings by blaming others. . . .*

 I've found that some of the small judgments I've leveled at situa- tions or other people have stemmed from some perception of inadequacy, fear, or doubt that is present in my own mind, and the judged person is only acting as a mirror to what's in myself. Most of the other judg- ments I make are a reflection of habit or behaviors, "the way I was taught to do things." When people or situations fall outside of these limits, small judgments occur, e.g., something that might go against my sense of fairness or equality.

* I can see now that my anger against those who don't push and fight and strive to be the best they can be is a frustrated desire within myself to sometimes "let go" and not have to always strive for perfection. . . . Connected to this is my sense of responsibility . . . and suffering with my first serious cold in over four years, I realize that until I had a serious sounding cough, weakened voice, and could barely think straight. . . . I could not give myself permission to slow down. . . . I realize that I had been letting work take over my life again and replace the healthier lifestyle habits I had been incorporating into my behaviors (e.g., meditation, regular exercise, leaving work earlier, not taking work home, adding "play" to my life). I also see that I am jealous of people who can relax and have fun and not feel guilty about not meeting (my expectations?!) of their responsibilities.

* Caring/showing affection: I get upset with people who do not show that they care. I believe that their actions should speak for themselves. Yet, I myself do not tell people often enough how much I care for them. I tend to reflect what I judge as unacceptable behavior towards me, back in my behavior towards them, or worse, distance myself from them before I get hurt. I do have difficulty showing kindness, caring, and compassion sometimes, because I feel it will make me vulnerable to being hurt. I have been bumped and bruised so many times in the past that I keep ever on guard to put up walls when I feel insecure. Rather than being true to myself by showing how I care for them in my own way, I modify my attitude. So I can see that I do project my own qualities in how I view others.

Exercises

1. Finding what we resent in others in ourselves

(a) Think of some qualities or attitudes in one or more other people that you resent (borrow from previous sessions' exercises if you like). Now try to find some evidence of these qualities in yourself. If you find yourself detesting or "attacking" some quality in another person, try to sense how you may be attacking it in yourself: "Part of me detests what another part is doing."

(b) If this is difficult, think rather of qualities or habits in others that irritate or frustrate you. Focus on the way these things make your life more uncomfortable. Now note whether or not you are to some extent blaming your discomfort on them. This is a form of projection—saying that *you* are the cause of my discomfort or inconvenience. Can you see how you could take back the responsibility for your own mental state by owning your reaction, and changing it?

(c) Think of (and write about) examples where you tell yourself, "I'm not getting what I need from this person or situation." Is this a projection of your own frustration with yourself, or with part of yourself?

2. Imagining yourself secure

(a) After relaxing deeply, imagine that you feel totally secure and fulfilled, universally liked and respected by other people, and by God. How does that feel inside?

(b) Now, continuing to be aware of this feeling, look back at one of the people or situations that you resented. Do they bother you now? This is potentially a very powerful exercise, which should be diligently explored. It can show us quite convincingly that our frustration with others depends on our dissatisfaction with ourselves. More than that, it can show us how our projection creates our world!

3. Attempting to stop judging others

This is a further version of exercises from the preceding chapters. Pick someone with whom you interact daily and towards whom you cherish some resentment. Resolve to try and drop this feeling. In your imagination, practice seeing them surrounded by light. Tell yourself that when you meet them you will have only one of many possible "channels" open—the one that allows love and understanding to flow between you. (The other channels, for hate, anger, fear, and other unpleasant emotions, remain closed.) Observe what your interactions are like over the week. Since there is only this "good" channel available, can the other person touch you with any negative emotions?

Meditation

The practice for this chapter is the silent repetition of a prayer, over a daily period of twenty to thirty minutes. A full description of this process can be found in many of the books by Eknath Easwaran, as part of his eight-point program. Easwaran has published a collection of poems suitable for this kind of meditation in *God Makes the Rivers to Flow*. One that he recommends is the "St. Francis Prayer," below. He suggests going through it very slowly, with a pause after each line, to allow it to sink in. Don't follow any association of ideas or try to think about the passage. If you can commit it to memory first, the process is even more effective. Or you can use it as a writing meditation, that is, writing it repeatedly with the mind calm and focused.

> *Lord, make me an instrument of thy peace.*
> *Where there is hatred, let me sow love;*
> *Where there is injury, pardon;*
> *Where there is doubt, faith;*
> *Where there is despair, hope;*
> *Where there is darkness, light;*
> *Where there is sadness, joy.*
>
> *O Divine Master, grant that I may not so much seek*
> *To be consoled as to console;*
> *To be understood as to understand;*
> *To be loved as to love;*
> *For it is in giving that we receive;*
> *It is in pardoning that we are pardoned;*
> *It is in dying to self that we are born to eternal life.*

As Easwaran says in *The Undiscovered Country,* we are not "addressing some extraterrestrial being outside. The kingdom of heaven is within us, and the Lord is enshrined in the depths of our own consciousness."

* *I used the familiar St. Francis Prayer; I can feel my appreciation for meditation growing as I practice it more often. Now instead of spending time during the session wondering "how much longer" I am actually surprised when the timer goes off to signal half an hour has passed. I also find myself looking forward to the peace and quiet of my meditation session rather than busying myself with other things just to put it off as I did in the beginning. Each time it seems that it is about halfway through the session that my mind really quietens down.*

8 | Extending Love

We all want to love and be loved. Yet there are few things about which more confusion exists than love. The word is used for many behaviors and states of mind, so our first task, as always, is to clarify what we mean. The exercises below are an important step towards this end, listing why we love some specific person. It can be painful to do this honestly, because we will find that a lot of what we assumed was love for another is in fact dependency (for comfort, security, status, sex, entertainment, and so on). That is, to put it bluntly, we tend to love others because of what we can get from them, which is not love but exploitation.

The mystics of all persuasions tell us that love is not about getting at all, it is only about giving. Love is blissful communion without any personal agenda—love without an object, or unconditional love. It can be felt for all living things, for God, for oneself, and perhaps is most often experienced in reasonably pure form between a parent and small child, or even toward a pet. It is the absence of separation between ourselves and the loved object. Love and joy are closely related.

Whenever you are not wholly joyous,
it is because you have reacted with a lack of love
to one of God's creations.

In fact, love is the very core of our being and is what we must extend to everyone else:

Teach only love, for that is what you are; and
Unless love's meaning is restored to you,
you cannot know yourself who share its meaning.
(*A Course in Miracles*)

How can we learn to love unconditionally? It is the same question as asking "How can I know my true nature?" or "How can I know God?" You will recall the four main paths we outlined early on in this book:

- *the path of understanding:* in this context, understanding what keeps us from love
- *the path of meditation:* removing all negative (and other) thoughts, so that we can be completely with another
- *the path of devotion:* deliberately cultivating loving feelings (for God)
- *the path of selfless service:* giving up the focus on self in order to express love for others through service.

As I've said earlier, we are focusing primarily on the path of understanding in this course, in order to progress as quickly as possible. We have discussed judgment of others, and seen that this is the outward projection of our own self-criticism and frustration. Clearly a first step toward learning to love is to stop this, and to accept responsibility for our own emotions and situations, rather than blaming others. Then we can turn to projecting positive emotions instead, even if it feels artificial. *A Course in Miracles* speaks of "extending," meaning letting love flow from ourselves toward all, abolishing the separation. Sending light to others, as in the Divine

Light Mantra exercise on page 94, is an example of extending, as is the exercise we did earlier on trying to see the person independent of his or her behavior.

Ultimately, we can love others fully only if we learn to love ourselves. We have to pursue what Easwaran calls "healing our own hearts and minds." This is a large task, and everything in this book, and in all spiritual systems, is ultimately about this healing of the self. Our true self-love will grow as we apply the techniques we have learned so far, understanding how we have been operating, then withdrawing the judgment and undoing the guilt. As we have seen, it is not so much a process of learning something new as of removing the obstacles to the expression of what is already there.

> Your task is not to seek for love, but merely to seek and find all of the barriers within yourself that you have built against it. (*A Course in Miracles*)

Learning to love is necessary if we are to feel true compassion for others. What the world feels for those in trouble tends to be, if anything, pity, which is a condescending sense of difference from them, tinged with fear and relief that "it's not my problem." Sympathy is another ambiguous word, meaning, literally, feeling along with another; this, too can become self-serving, an indulgence in one's own emotional needs. Compassion is, by contrast, more emotionally detached; someone is in trouble, we feel only love for them, based on equality, and extend to them the healing love we would ourselves receive.

Ultimately, according to the spiritual masters, all true love is for the Divine, and this love spills over on to other people. We are engaged, then, in developing a "love affair" with God or the Divine. We need to foster this with all our available energies, to engage in what is more conventionally called "worship," not because God needs our adulation, but because we need to learn to express it. The path of *devotion* emphasizes this process: finding an avatar or person who has fully realized the Divine (such as Jesus, Krishna, Divine Mother, or the Buddha) or other symbols of the Divine, setting up an altar, and transmuting our emotional forces into spiritual energy. This path is common in India, where there are very many symbols—gods and goddesses—representing the underlying Divine Mind. It can mesh well with the practice of seeking understanding. If you are attracted to the path of devotion, then you may need to find a human figure, often Jesus, or one of the Indian avatars to and for whom you can express this love. Or you may find that you can worship God as a living spirit. There is a longstanding debate in Eastern spiritual writings, on whether God "has form" or is "without form." It is not a question we can answer because of our limited human understanding. In practical terms, I would suggest we imagine God or the Divine in whatever way works for us.

What our patients have written

* *(writing for Exercise 1a) Love is acceptance of another person and I think unconditional love is total acceptance. I believe that the only way you can accept someone else is to accept yourself. Love is something you share with the world. I feel loved when I feel totally accepted. I have sisters and I know they love me unconditionally. They don't care what I look like or what I do, they love me.*

   Love also means wanting to take burdens away from others and shouldering them yourself. That's the love that I have for my children and others in my family. Conditional love is a power trip. It assumes that love is finite and that you have to get yours at the expense of someone else. Unconditional love has no bounds or limits. There's enough to go around and it's self-producing. The more we express unconditional love the more of it there is in this world.

(Exercise 1b) I love you because:

- *You provide for me*
- *You are honorable*
- *You stand by me during all my physical trials*
- *You give me space to follow my path*

- *You're easygoing*
- *You're a loving father*
- *You're understanding*
- *You're funny*
- *You're undemanding*
- *You're happy*
- *You like to have fun*
- *You keep me company*

I recognize that a lot of the things above are my own personal agenda, things I want or need from the relationship. Believe it or not, I find it harder to unconditionally love my closest relationships, which is odd because these are the people I love the most. I don't have an agenda when it comes to my neighbor, but I do when it comes to my husband or kids.

* *Unconditional love, is, I think, a lot of what I feel for my children. I don't mean to say that I've never been angry with them, but that I always love them, even when they behave in ways that might be considered annoying, or not very nice. I'm always clear on the fact that first and foremost I love them. I think that part of the reason that I can feel this way about them is that my love for them is not dependent on getting something back from them, which is not to say that getting something back isn't wonderful. It's just that my love doesn't depend on that. My love for them doesn't come from the relationship, but from deep inside me.*

* *What is Love?*

- *giving: overflowing, expression of vitality*
- *power: which produces love*
- *caring: active concern for the life that we love*
- *responsibility: able and ready to respond*
- *respectful: aware of unique individuality*
- *knowledgeable: "know thyself"*

Spiritual Love

- *Right action as described in the Buddhist "Noble Eightfold Path"*
- *"Choose only love"*
- *Non-attachment to the outcome*

It would be wonderful to be able to love every creature in this way. The expansiveness and freedom in the acceptance of "what is" in ourselves and others.

Exercises

1. Investigating love

(a) What is love? Write down your thoughts generally. If it's difficult, think of all the behaviors you associate with loving.

(b) Considering your most important love relationship (likely to be your spouse or partner, but could be a child or very good friend), set up a series of answers to yourself in the form "I love you because . . ." (you accept me, look after me, entertain me, etc.). List all the reasons you can think of.

(c) How does "spiritual" or "unconditional" love differ from worldly love? What would be the effects of loving others in this way? On them? On yourself?

2. Creating a "sacred space"

If you have not already done so, make yourself a space at home that is dedicated to your regular meditation or prayer. It should include some kind of small table on which you can put any objects that would help you focus on the spiritual work as you sit in front of it. These might include statues of spiritual figures, pictures (in stand-alone frames), flowers, incense, candles, or any other meaningful objects. Ideally this will stand in a room dedicated to spiritual practice, but if this is not possible, find some way of closing it off when not in use, for example, with movable screens.

What do you think about the possibility and relevance of making your mind a "sacred space" or receptacle for the Divine? Can you invoke, during your prayer of meditation, a sense of intense love or devotion towards the Divine, or a symbol of it, like Christ or Divine Mother? What are the problems or resistances you encounter within yourself to these ideas? Do you encounter scorn or other negative reactions from others who are important to you?

3. Prayer

Prayer is an important part of worship. In its most elementary form, it can be seen as asking for what we want, yet most of us would have some unease about this, and might want to consider more carefully what our prayer should be.

As a supplement to *A Course in Miracles*, two further small books were "channeled": *Psychotherapy: Purpose, Process, and Practice*, and *The Song of Prayer: Prayer, Forgiveness, Healing*. Consider this extract from *The Song of Prayer*:

> Prayer is a stepping aside; a letting go, a quiet time of listening and loving. It should not be confused with supplication of any kind, because it is a way of remembering your holiness. Why should holiness entreat, being fully entitled to everything Love has to offer? And it is to love you go in prayer. Prayer is an offering; a giving up of yourself to be at one with Love. There is nothing to ask because there is nothing left to want. That nothingness becomes the altar of God. It disappears in Him.

How does this compare with your own ideas about prayer? What do you think prayer is? If you are asking for something, who are you asking, and why?

The Practice of the Presence of God is a delightful and classic little work written mainly by Brother Lawrence, a seventeenth-century monk, whose simple discipline (!) it was to try to think always of the Divine, i.e., to pray. It is well worthwhile to read this book. If you do read it, ask yourself how his recommendations compare with those in *The Song of Prayer*.

For the next week or so, as well as your meditation, you might like to include prayer in your daily practice. Write some notes on your experience, and consider whether you want to include prayer as part of your regular spiritual healing work.

9 | Self-Preoccupation, Self-Will, and Surrender

We look around and see other people and things as if from a central point of observation. We seem to be the center of our world, much as the Earth seemed, before Galileo, to be the center of the universe. As we grow from childhood we learn some limits to our self-importance, but the private impression of self-centerdness remains at some level. As a dying patient once said to me, "I can't imagine the world without me in it."

This self-preoccupation or sense of personal specialness generates various problems. For example, it seems to confer entitlement to all kinds of privileges: to health, long life, a degree of prosperity and comfort, and so on, with variations according to our cultural upbringing. Inevitably, some of these desires are frustrated, giving rise to the inner conflict that we call unhappiness. To counter this, we try to change things around ourselves, but as sages East and West have long pointed out, this is difficult, and in the end, irrelevant. We can't change the world to any great extent, we can change only ourselves—our reaction to events.

An even more fundamental problem with living life as a special being is that it obscures our true identity. In fact, what we identify with can be seen as the main issue in spiritual growth and healing. The choice is between being a separate entity locked in a struggle to get what one wants from the world, or an identity as a small part of something infinitely larger, a Cosmic Mind perhaps. As Easwaran puts it in *Original Goodness*:

> In the end, the goal of all spiritual seeking is to live in this state of self-forgetfulness permanently. This continuous awareness of God is to be achieved not after death, but here and now; that is what brings heaven on earth. . . . The Lord's Prayer says plainly, "Thy will be done." But before His will can be done, our will—self-will—has to go. William Law put it precisely: "To sum up all in a word: nothing hath separated us from God but our own will, or rather our own will is our separation from God." Here again we must remember that words like "Lord" and "God" do not refer to some higher being in another galaxy. We are talking about a barrier that separates us from our own deepest self, the very source and ground of what makes us human and gives meaning to our lives.

The prospect of such a shift in identification can be profoundly unsettling to our egos; our minds turn immediately to what we would have to "give up." Our whole Western culture is based on the idea that our individuality is somehow special and sacred. Yet, what if we could "look down" at ourselves from a detached viewpoint, much as an adult might look at small children throwing tantrums in a schoolyard; or (as beings from another galaxy might) as small fish in a school of millions of the same species? Might not our insistence on our individual importance look ridiculous? Here is an another excerpt from *A Course in Miracles*:

> This fragment of your mind is such a tiny part of it that, could you but appreciate the whole, you would see instantly that it is like the smallest sunbeam to the sun, or like the faintest ripple on the surface of the ocean. In its amazing arrogance, this tiny sunbeam has decided it is the sun; this almost imperceptible

ripple hails itself as the ocean. Think how alone and frightened is this little thought, this infinitesimal illusion, holding itself apart against the universe. . . . Do not accept this little, fenced-off aspect as yourself. The sun and ocean are as nothing beside what you are.

In other words, we are advised to submerge ourselves in the larger whole, or God, and give up the childish insistence on complete autonomy. This is the often misunderstood concept of spiritual "surrender," which can sound supine, but which, as anyone who has made the slightest effort in this direction will attest, is an intensely active process and perhaps the toughest challenge we can ever face. The promise is that as we learn to "let go and let God," to allow ourselves to be guided rather than insisting on control, we will begin to experience the peace and healing that comes with an awareness of our true identity. Far from losing ourselves, we will find we are much more than we imagined. Our lives will begin to take directions that benefit ourselves and those around us. There is no suggestion that we should abandon activity; instead, we are asked to give up our emotional investment in or attachment to our different roles, placing ourselves at the service of the Divine. A better word than surrender may be non-attachment, since the essence of the process is to continue to act, but without emotional investment in the outcomes of our actions—that is left to God.

You will find this concept everywhere in whatever spiritual tradition you read. It needs careful, slow turning over in one's mind, and experimentation in our own lives. In Chapter 6 we briefly explored the negative face of self-image—our tendency toward guilt. In this chapter we are beginning to look at the self in an alternative and intensely positive way: as a small part of a magnificent whole. Please note that none of this means we are not important or that we don't matter to the Divine. Again, the spiritual traditions all emphasize that we each have our part to play. We could visualize ourselves as pieces of a giant jigsaw puzzle, a whole that would be spoiled by the absence of even one piece. Note also that this is not a moral question we are discussing, but a matter of ultimate identity. Of course it is important to be considerate to others, to "do as we would be done by," but underlying that is the much more fundamental issue of how we view ourselves in relationship to others, and to the world. Highly moral behavior can be very selfish, as when we do good works to look good or boost a flagging self-esteem. Some religions, such as Christianity, emphasize the importance of the individual; others, like Buddhism, say there is no separate "self." I don't think these views are as opposite as they may first appear. We can reconcile them by concentrating on how our experience shifts, with spiritual practice, from a sense of total separateness to at least occasional flashes of being part of something much more grand.

The diagram on page 126 (Figure 9.1) was drawn up as a result of discussions in one of our classes, showing some of the consequences of an insistence on our personal importance, and a route to returning to communion with the Divine through forgiveness.

What our patients have written

* *Roles have different purposes. Some are for growth, some are for fun, some are for others. Can I perform a role like mothering without being emotionally attached to the outcome? That's pretty hard. Perhaps I should just be trying to do my best and leave the rest to God. I try to do that, but it is difficult.*

* *(writing for Exercise 1): My roles in priority from most important:*

  • *Spiritual quester—being, not doing: This is my life's focus now and my other roles have faded into the background. If I were an Indian man I would now be on my spiritual "walkabout" having completed my obligations to my family.*
  • *Mother: My children are grown, self-sufficient, leading their own lives, and my relationship with them is loving. I am available to give help or advice if asked just as they are available to me.*
  • *Friend: Closeness without neediness.*

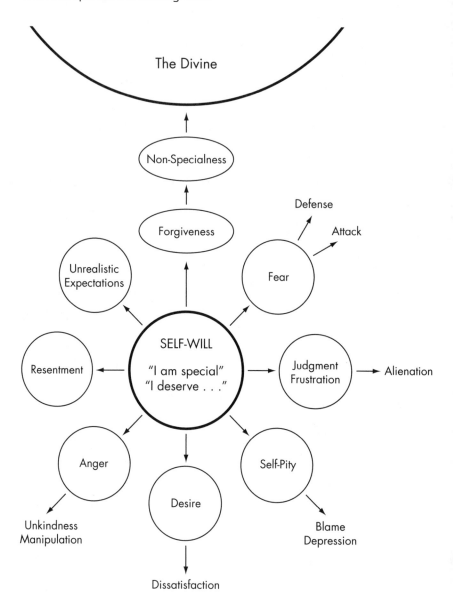

Figure 9.1
Results of self-will, when expressed or diminished—a group discussion.

- *Cancer patient: Has become less and less of a role—just is a statement about what is.*
- *Unemployed: My job was "out-sourced" about four months before I was diagnosed, which stopped all plans for finding another similar position. I am grateful for those four months of "doing nothing" and thank providence for providing that downtime.*

My life is quite simple now and I can't think of any other roles that I play although I know that I can enter into roles if I choose to. It is rather like playing a character in a play—but I am always aware that I am playing a part. I look on this type of role-playing as a means of functioning and getting things done in this society. Once again, I don't think that the issue is giving up roles but rather being unattached to them.

* *(responding to Exercise 2) Last night I practiced three hours of silence with [partner and daughter]. They both felt very uncomfortable with me being silent. [He] felt that he had to be silent too, and [she] felt very insecure with me not talking. By the end of the three hours, she was in tears because I couldn't talk to her. I found it quite freeing. I felt as though I was there, but I was also very detached from what was going on. My silence allowed me to give up two roles that I usually play, that of the pleaser and that of the mediator. Being unable to talk, I wasn't able to cater to anyone, because I couldn't ask the two of them what they wanted. They had to fare for themselves. [She] is quite emotional, and she usually gets upset with [him] for one reason or another when they are playing. I usually step in and talk to her about it and try to resolve the dispute. When she got upset last night, I couldn't talk to her, so I just gave her a hug, and let her come around in her own time to being friends with [him] again. Without my help, she settled her disputes with him quite easily. I realized that they don't need me to play that role, they are quite capable of doing it themselves. When I think about this, I realize how controlling I am. In my effort to make sure everyone is happy, I try to control their actions, instead of just letting them flow. I always thought of this as trying to please, but it really is an attempt to control.*

* *I see myself as a tiny part of a vast web of life that is connected to a higher power. Now I realize that at times my sense of who I am in this web is greatly inflated—when I'm absorbed in my own worries and anxieties I tend to lose my sense of myself in relation to the larger universe. It's as if my existence is composed of many, many layers, including the collection of memories of moments in my life, events, feelings, dramas, fears, etc. When I notice this and am able to strip away or discard these layers, I can begin to picture myself as just a tiny particle, connected to this vast web of life on earth, and I can imagine, in a very crude way, how this web of life is just a tiny speck in an infinite universe. When I "fix" my sense of self to the many things that make up my sense of identity, then this sense of self takes up much more of my consciousness. For example, when I think of myself as a wife, mother, daughter, sister, etc., then I have all kinds of thoughts related to my life with the people I love. Sometimes these thoughts (memories, hopes, worries, etc.) consume my awareness and I become swept away by feelings of sadness, and fear of loss related to these people. When I am able to transcend this sense of identity and picture myself as just a minute part of a vast universe, then I can be more detached as I look down at myself in daily life and am less swept away by my usual worries.*

Exercises

1. Giving up our roles

(a) Get a number of small pieces of paper of equal size (for example, by tearing standard sheets into eight or twelve pieces), and on each piece, write one of the roles you play in life, e.g., wife, father, part-time volunteer, accountant, student, teacher, etc. Include words describing parts that you play as a result of your personality: authority figure, life of the party, wet blanket, and so on. Have you included any that describe your spiritual seeking?

(b) Now lay these out and assign a priority to each. Then stack them in order. Then start discarding, from the bottom of the order (the least-valued role), pausing to reflect as you think that you are giving up that function. As the pile shrinks, and you reach the last few attributes or roles, watch your mind carefully. Consider what you think would be the impact of dropping these roles on the meaningfulness and pleasure of your life.

(c) Write about this. What was most difficult to "give up" and why? Can you continue to act in your various roles with less attachment to them?

2: Practice of Silence

Mahatma Gandhi observed a period of silence every day, which he would not break for anyone, not even the most important of visiting statesmen. When we are voluntarily silent for a time we begin to understand a number of important things, for example, how we use energy in speaking, how others may relate to our words rather than to who we are, and how our self-image depends on being able to justify ourselves. For this exercise, choose a period when you would normally be interacting with others, explain to them what you are doing, and maintain silence for a time ranging from three hours to twenty-four hours or more. Write about what you learn.

3. Imagery of subpersonalities

We can think of our personalities as being made up of a number of "individuals" each with its own particular qualities. Thus we might have an "inner child" (thought patterns that were active in childhood), an "inner critic" (that part of ourselves, perhaps an "internalized parent," that constantly judges what we do, a "bold explorer," a "romantic," "a sensitive artist," a "hard worker," and a "wimp."

(a) After relaxing deeply, allow an image to come up that seems to represent a part of yourself. See if you can give it a name. Perhaps you can even talk to it, as you may have done in the past with the Inner Healer (who is also a part of us). If you do get a reasonably clear image, draw it and write a description. Visit this image again next week and in subsequent weeks, and note changes.

(b) If this seems to work for you, you may be able to generate and identify a number of such subpersonalities. Are there one or more that seem to have a "spiritual" flavor? If ideas and images are slow in coming, help them along with your conscious ideas. Think about your main activities and how you tend to behave while performing them, and see if a picture, however vague and fanciful, comes to mind. For example, if you tend to be a controlling person in your environment, you might summon up an image of an authoritarian figure, perhaps exaggerated.

As background for this work it would be helpful to read about a kind of therapy called "psychosynthesis." It's described in Roberto Assagioli's *Psychosynthesis*, and in books by Alice Epstein and Robert Elliott. (See the Reading List at the end of this book.)

4. Our sense of being cared for

Read the well-known "Footprints" story, below. Then, in a deeply relaxed state, imagine yourself as being carried by the Lord through a difficult period of your life, perhaps through the experience of cancer. You can vary the imagery by imagining walking across a desert plain until you reach a huge statue of the Buddha, which you enter through a side door, and, climbing up many steps, emerge into the "cradle" formed by his hands held in front of his body. Lie there, imagining yourself held in total love and security. Write about either experience.

Footprints
One night a man had a dream. He dreamed he was walking along the beach with the Lord. Across the sky flashed scenes from his life. For each scene he noticed two sets of footprints in the sand—one belonging to him and the other to the Lord.

When the last scene of his life flashed before him, he looked back at the footprints in the sand. He noticed that many times along the path of his life there was only one set of footprints. He also noticed that this happened during the lowest and saddest times in his life.

This really bothered him and he questioned the Lord about it. "Lord, you said that once I decided to follow you,

you would walk with me all the way. But I noticed that during the most troublesome times in my life, there is only one set of footprints. I don't understand why, when I needed you most, you deserted me."

The Lord replied, "My precious, precious child, I love you and I would never leave you. During your times of trial and suffering when you see only one set of footprints, it was then that I carried you."

AUTHOR UNKNOWN

Meditation

If you haven't already done so, choose one of the methods you have learned for continuing daily practice. It will also be valuable for you to continue the mind watching from time to time, until it becomes a regular habit to monitor your thoughts.

10 | Desire and Acceptance

We are largely driven by our desires: for comfort, first of all, meaning freedom from pain, a full belly, warmth, shelter, security, and sex; then with these basic "needs" satisfied, for a degree of control over events, and for stimulation or diversion. We take this for granted—what else would we do? And is there something wrong with this?

Such a central assumption in our lives needs investigation if we are serious about the spiritual path. The list above could be equally well applied to the motivation of an intelligent animal like a dog. The questions we need to ask ourselves are, "Is that all? Is there something more?" The problem with being completely driven by desire is that it will keep us at the "animal" level of development. There is a famous passage from the *Upanishads*, an ancient Indian text:

> You are what your deep, driving desire is.
> As your deep, driving desire is, so is your will.
> As your will is, so is your deed.
> As your deed is, so is your destiny.

In other words, we become what we desire. If it's food, we may become obese. If money, we may become rich, and if power, then we are likely to gain control over others. All of these accomplishments have a cost. And the desire is frequently frustrated, leading to unhappiness.

The spiritual traditions all propose an opposite course to the pursuit of satisfaction of our desires, namely, to try to free ourselves from desire. They point out that attachments of any kind are imprisoning—we can all see, in the modern world, how our superabundance of possessions can become a trap, and in a similar way, how an obsession with some kind of personal accomplishment (e.g., the drive to make money) can stunt our lives. It is not that there is anything wrong with pleasure, they point out, simply that it is irrelevant, and its pursuit distracts us from the spiritual goal of finding meaning in relationship to a larger whole.

This sounds very foreign, at first, to the modern Western person, who has probably been conditioned since early childhood to strive toward the related goals of becoming special (Chapter 9) and accomplishing a series of self-determined and societally sanctioned objectives. "If I'm not feeding my desires, what fun would there be in life?" The answer of the scriptures is that true joy will not be known until personal desire is mastered. As stated in *A Course in Miracles*:

> I sought for many things, and found despair.
> Now do I seek but one,
> for in that one is all I need, and only what I need.
> All that I sought before I needed not, and did not even want.
> My only need I did not recognize.
> But now I see that I need only truth.
> In that all needs are satisfied, all cravings end, all hopes are
> finally fulfilled and dreams are gone.
> Now I have everything I could need.
> Now I have everything that I could want.
> And now at last I find myself at peace.

As usual, the goal seems lofty and impossibly distant. What can we ordinary people do as a first step? Think back to Chapter 4, on judgment, and recall how busy our minds are, most of the time, judging other people and situations. We always seem to *want* something different from what we are currently experiencing—if you still don't believe it, you will need to do more work, checking this out by close attention to the mind. This constant wanting, naturally, breeds discontent. The Buddhist texts, in particular, are very clear on the misery this generates. So this suggests our first step: can we become aware of the clamor of our desires and try to suspend them? Can we replace the constant dissatisfaction with events or people by an *acceptance* of what is, of whatever set of circumstances we find ourselves in? Can we focus precisely on the present moment, rather than the past or the future? The *Tao Te Ching*, a central text of the Taoist religion, has this to say:

> There is no greater sin than desire,
> No greater curse than discontent,
> No greater misfortune than wanting something for oneself.
> Therefore he who knows that enough is enough
> will always have enough.

What our patients have written

* (in response to Exercise 1)

Wants	What would be lost by giving it up	What would be gained
To be more efficient at work	Very little—it is an illusion that I need to be	Less stress
To give up work	Basic living expenses, boredom	Less stress: explore other interests
To give up playing computer games	None really (stress reliever)	More time to do more meaningful things

Wants	What would be lost by giving it up	What would be gained
Good income	Simple pleasure	Pressure decreased to conform to expected lifestyle
Work on educational projects	Opportunity to share expertise	Time for other pursuits
More money, less debt	Nothing would be lost by giving up this desire	Less stress over my financial situation

* (in response to Exercise 2)

My Ideals	Modifying Comments
To appear more intelligent to my friends	I might just be myself and think for myself
To not make mistakes at work	Just correct them, everybody makes them— don't beat up on yourself!
I must be independent and strong	I define my strength as independence. Maybe I need to change my situation. I need to find a definition of strength that allows others in.
I must say yes when others ask for my help	I enjoy helping others, but if I feel that I must help, not that I want to help, then I will be helping with resentment. If I am too tired, or helping will place an undue burden on me, I must learn to say no without feeling guilty.

* I don't see that desire is the trap (negative) but that it is (1) being unable to distinguish need from want. When I can recognize wanting it becomes part of the spiritual journey. It's (2) to detach from the goal of wanting and is far more humanly attainable than detaching from desire. It means I don't have to get what I want. I'm not attached to the outcome. I just watch the wanting mind and practice. I see my needs. I see my wants. I can or don't let them move me. (3) It's my choice.

* Perhaps acceptance is to live with our desires, needs, and wants, just as they are. They do not have to be attached to behaviors. It's our choice.

Exercises

1. Distinguishing "wants" from "needs"

It is easy to confuse these two, and we are all very skilled at rationalizing our wants. So to put ourselves on the spot, try an exercise like the following. List your wants, in all aspects of life, in a column, then check in an adjacent column which of them is, in fact, a need. You might use as system like "2" means definite need, "1" a small need, and "0" means not really needed. It should be quite easy to find thirty or more. This process of analysis could then be extended by listing the pros and cons of giving up those wants that are not needed:

Wants	Needs	What would be lost by giving it up	What would be gained
Basic nutrition	2	Not applicable	
High-fat desserts	0	Immediate satisfaction	Slimmer, healthier body
Accomplishing more at work	1	Very little in fact	Stress would be eased, and more time freed up, with less emphasis on work
and so on . . .			

2. Our cherished ideals

As an adjunct to Exercise 1, make a list of your most cherished ideals about yourself, how you must look and act, what you must accomplish (e.g., "I must always be smartly dressed when seen in public"; "I must earn the respect of my colleagues at work"; "I must keep my husband/wife happy"). This list could also be very long if you do it conscientiously. Then against each item, write a modifying comment, after reflection (e.g., "I aim to please my spouse, but his happiness is his own responsibility," and so on).

3. Fasting

One area where the power of desire is exposed rather starkly is in eating and drinking. We have all had to make choices between what tastes good and what we believe is nutritious for ourselves. It would be fair to say that we have some degree of "addiction" to food, meaning that we are preoccupied with the pleasure of eating beyond that necessary to sustain life. This is a habit we learned early, and develop further during life as we associate eating with the delights of a varied and tasty diet.

As with all our habits we need to investigate this one. Fasting is one way to do this—it sharpens our awareness of why we seek sensations from food, over and above supporting our bodies. A simple version of this exercise is to forgo an evening meal. Notice how your body reacts to missing the expected food and, more important, notice your thoughts and feelings before, during and after this. You may heighten the experience by observing others eat while you do not.

A more demanding level of the exercise is to fast for twenty-four hours or more, taking only water or perhaps fruit juices, and recording the same observations. Write about your own urge to eat. How much of it is habit and desire for taste sensations, diversion, a feeling of fullness in the stomach (i.e., comfort), social interaction, or other ends? What would be, for you, an optimal degree of control over what you eat?

Meditation

I hope that by now you are continuing your meditation as a routine. It's an excellent idea to read some of the many books about it, to give you some perspective, but nothing can substitute for the actual practice!

11 | Living a More Spiritual Life

It is time to put together what we have learned and consider how we want to conduct our lives from here on. Reading about spirituality is important, but in the end it is action that matters—action that takes place primarily in the mind. How can I live a more spiritual life? What is it important that I do?

The first decision is about priorities. To heal spiritually, and hence psychologically and physically, this must be the top priority in life, in the same way as making money would need to be the top priority of someone who wanted to get rich quickly. We tend to think immediately of what this would require us to "give up," which weakens resolve. So if you are persuaded that spiritual growth and healing is important, start by affirming frequently that this is your top concern, at least for the next couple of years (after which you will not have any ambivalence about it). Swami Radha used to point out that people readily accept the need to spend five to ten years or more training for a career; why not put the same amount of effort into something even more important, like finding our true nature?

Another way of defining your priorities is to ask, "With what do I want to identify?" Is our identity simply that of a biological animal, living a basically pointless life on this earth, then disappearing forever, or can we discover our identity as an eternal, non-material being, part of an immensely larger framework or Intelligence? In other words, do our lives have meaning? Is the point of our lives simply to have as much pleasure or comfort as possible, or is it to find this meaning?

Having decided to "go for it," what then? In the most general terms, our task is to become as *aware* as possible. When the Buddha was asked what he was—was he a saint? a god? and so on—he is reputed to have replied, "I am awake." What does being awake or aware mean? It means, initially, trying to know what is going on in our minds at all times. You will be aware by now of the stream of judgment and commentary on oneself and others that constitutes most mental life. Being aware gives us the option of changing this self-talk. We can then replace it with a degree of quiet, and/or with more helpful ideas, such as "choose only love." This can extend into the most mundane areas. For example, rather than feeling bored with our daily functions and tasks, with our environment, friends, and colleagues, we can cultivate gratitude and interest, awareness of all that has gone into providing us with food, for example, interest in the ever-changing patterns of weather or gratitude that our bowels are working!

The next attribute to consider, having decided to make spiritual development a priority and to cultivate awareness, might be dedication. This lies a little downstream, as it were, from setting priorities, and refers to the actions we take, clearing a space for the task. It helps, and is probably essential, to simplify life as much as possible to leave room for spiritual exercises. While the point is, ultimately, to spiritualize everything we do, so that outward actions need not differ at all from the ordinary, most of us need plenty of time dedicated to meditation, reading, and reflection, separate from the routine events of life. So consider how you can simplify. What can go? Can you let go of TV and other media? Some of the pointless socializing that takes so much time and energy? Some of the excess time spent at work?

Having "set the scene" with an appropriate attitude to the spiritual healing journey, we then ask ourselves what specific techniques we will employ. Here schools of thought differ somewhat, but the methods we use may not matter as much as the dedication with which we pursue them. Eastern systems of spiritual education are often far more demanding than anything we are accustomed to in the West. However, other teachers have come from India and adapted these methods to the Western mind (making them less severe!). An example is the eight-point program of Eknath Easwaran, which you will find in many of his books.

We can list some basic processes that are common to most systems of spiritual evolution. Most of this repeats what has been said earlier in this book:

- **Developing understanding**: This comes from reading and discussion, and particularly from conscientiously examining the application of spiritual insights to our own lives. This book has attempted to convey the most important ideas.

- **Quietening the mind**: Having explored our obstacles with reason, we then need to drop the compulsive thinking, and *listen*, meaning to be aware, through the senses, of what our physical organism is doing, and even more important, trying to be aware of the Divine within. Meditation in its various forms is the classical discipline for cultivating this listening faculty.

- **Affirmation**: Putting into our minds what we want to become. Easwaran recommends this strongly (see the Reading List), and his preferred method of meditation is to repeat the lines of inspirational passages and prayers, without editorializing. I have suggested here that we can say to ourselves, in all situations, "(I will) choose only love." You may have seen, if you have consulted *A Course in Miracles*, that it includes 365 daily exercises that are essentially affirmations to seed into our minds. This could become a course of continuing self-study for you once you've completed the exercises in this book.

- **Attending to relationships**: Other people and events provide opportunities to practice the attitudes of non-judgmental acceptance and eventually to understand that we are not separate, but at one with all living things.

- **A continuing dialogue with the Divine?** This is what the great sages tell us is possible—and desirable. Gary Zukav, in his excellent and forthright book *The Seat of the Soul,* says we need to "enter into a partnership with the Divine Intelligence." At some stage we do need to go beyond exploration and quietening the mind, and make a decision, involving an act of faith, that there is a larger Intelligence or God, and that our task is to find out what we are meant to do according to this Divine Order, while dropping our separate personal agendas.

This is a place to comment on two further, related techniques advocated within many spiritual and religious traditions. The first is listening to an "inner voice" or to "God's voice." It is the experience of many sincere seekers (myself included) that "messages" will come if we are open to receiving them. The difficulty is to distinguish this genuine "higher" communication from the self-serving voice of the ego. It is probably rare for communication to be in a form like human speech, although this does happen. More commonly, answers to questions and problems we may have are provided through other means—what other people say, in our dreams, and symbolic answers in the form of events around us.

This leads to the second and related point about communication with the transcendent order. If we are spiritually sincere, events in our lives come to have meaning, to answer questions, and to provide direction and teaching. A simple example would be a headache, which can teach the sufferer to slow down and pay attention to his or her behaviors. It is not that some divine parent manipulates things such that we are provided with salutary difficulties in life; rather, our perceptions of and projections upon the world create, usually unconsciously, what we need to further our growth. We can choose to examine, and indeed construct, the symbolic meaning of everything that happens to us. But it is not all our own creation. At some point we will experience the Universe "reaching down" to help us. One of the benefits of life-threatening disease is that we may be much more open to receiving this kind of help and support than at other times.

If you are serious about your spiritual work, your interests and attitudes may change considerably. While this will often improve your relationships with other people, some, especially those close to you, may not like these changes. They may, for example, feel guilty or inadequate if you are doing what they secretly feel they "ought" to do. You may be less interested in some former joint activities, such as watching movies. You will become much more sensitive to the motives underlying the actions of others, and when they realize this, it can provoke discomfort, even anger. It has to be said that if one partner becomes dedicated to spiritual work while the other does not, this can place a strain on the marriage. I can only suggest being very alert for the impact your study may be having on your relationships. Explain to your family what you are doing, and how important it is to you. Don't hold forth about what you are doing to others—your work and experiences, your enthusiasm for it even, should be kept relatively private. Talking about it a lot, or worse, trying to convert them, is irritating to most people. Practice forgiveness of them for their old, perhaps previously unobjectionable habits.

What our patients have written

* Today, I work fifteen hours a week [instead of sixty], and I do a number of activities that are centered only on me. I have very little pressure in my life, and what pressure I do have, I now have techniques for releasing. I think about my feelings, I worry about me, I am grateful for every day, and I have developed a wonderful spiritual connection. I am at peace with myself and the life that I now have. To a great extent, I have been able to put my past behind me. I am more loving, compassionate and tolerant than I ever knew I could be. I am a lucky lady!

* Cancer has accelerated the process of looking at the meaning of life. Exploring our individual role as part of the whole is something I don't think I would have pursued with such determination. Cancer has also taught me much about peace and that lovely safe place within.

* At the current point in my life the adventure of self-discovery, as well as discovering all the new avenues to which I am being exposed, fills me with awe, and I have an extremely strong desire to continue in this direction. . . . the techniques I am currently incorporating into my lifestyle fill me with joy and contentment.

* I feel certain that I will continue this healing work, at deeper levels, for the rest of my life, regardless of the state of my health or external variables. This healing work has helped me to experience life in a deeper and more fulfilling way, and it is clear to me that there is no limit to this depth as long as I stay involved in the process, i.e., as a lifelong process. I'm very grateful to have been able to find more meaning in my life—the healing work has been a motivator and a vehicle for me to do this.

My spiritual development has become a primary focus in my life. I don't see it as a separate category, but something integral to my life and part of everything I do. The more deeply I've become involved in spiritual practice, the more effortless it seems to lead a spiritual life. I don't mean "effortless" in the sense that it isn't hard work, but rather that a spiritual focus or outlook comes to me more naturally now than in the past. My spiritual development is the most important thing now in my life, because it affects so strongly how I am living each day, and also because it prepares me to accept my own death when the time comes.

Exercises

Since this is the last "working session" of the book, I have listed a number of exercises that could, if necessary, be spread over a prolonged period. Some version of the "Action Plan" (Exercise 3) should, however, be done in a thorough fashion in the near future, if you are serious about moving on with your self-healing.

1. "Mechanical" behavior
(a) List the things that you do during the day in a mechanical or unaware fashion, starting with getting up in the morning,

bathroom, breakfast, and continuing through the day. Against some of these, write down affirmations or ideas that you could encourage in your mind as aids to appreciating and fully experiencing these events. (Thich Nhat Hanh's books contain wonderful advice on how to be more "mindful" in our daily lives.)

(b) Next, list some of the mechanical or automatic reactions that you have to common situations. There are hundreds of these in everyday life, for example:

- "I hate it when the weather is . . ."
- "I always feel tired at the end of the day."
- "I am always afraid of . . ."
- "I can't stand to be bored . . ."
- "I don't like people who . . ."
- "I need to eat whenever . . ."
- "If I don't get my eight hours of sleep I . . ."
- "It's not fair to ask someone to . . ."

What have you learned from this? What can you do about it?

2. Goals revisited

Carry out the imaginary exercise, in a relaxed state, of looking back at your younger self at a number of different stages in your life, e.g., ten, twenty, thirty, forty, and fifty years ago (depending on your present age). If you could give this younger self advice, today, what would you tell him or her? What should he or she make the direction of her life? Can you move in this direction now?

3. Setting out an action plan

There are many ways to do this, and you may prefer to develop your own, but the important thing is to translate new understandings into action. One possible way is to go through the five "levels" of a person that were described in Chapter 2 (body, conscious mind, deeper mind, social, and spiritual), and set down the changes you need to make at each level, according to a scheme like the one below:

Current habits: What I do each day?

*What is it about this pattern that is
not ideal? What keeps me stuck in this?*

*What would be an ideal, although
realistic, practice for me daily?
What benefits do I expect from this?*

*What is the first step toward the
changes I want to make?*

*How will I counteract the obstacles
(resistances, old habits) that I encounter?*

Review also the things you have learned in this book, and in any others that you may have read, as you set out an action plan for yourself for the coming months. Be sure to include the "staples" in it: regular writing (in a journal), daily reflection and meditation, mind watching, and at least one of the "body awareness" disciplines (deep relaxation, hatha yoga, tai chi, or chi gong).

4. Attending a spiritual service
Attend some community spiritual activities. These could be church services (if you are not in the habit of going to church), a meditation group, or group meetings to study scriptural writings. Pick something that you think may challenge and extend your ideas. Write about the experience.

5. Dream analysis
Dreams provide a "window" into parts of the mind that are not normally accessible to us. We all dream and can learn to catch our dreams. Tell yourself before you go to sleep that you intend to wake after a dream and record it and have paper and pen, plus a suitable light, readily available by the bed. When you wake, keep your movements to a minimum and immediately write down as much as

you can remember. The feelings aroused are important, and need to be noted. Put down any impressions about the meaning of the dream at that time. Then return to sleep.

In the morning, you can analyze your dream by going through it and underlining all the words and phrases that seem significant, and noting especially all the symbols in the dream—the individuals, setting, objects, and events all symbolize something. Then consider each of these in turn, letting any associations that you have to the word come to your awareness. Write these down. When this listing is finished, go through the whole account. You may then find that some of the alternative meanings of the words or symbols you have used provide an explanation of the dream-play that was not originally obvious.

For the keen student, dream analysis can become part of the repertoire of techniques for self-understanding. You will probably need to read one of the many available books on the subject. There are various systems, so you may wish to explore several approaches to find what suits you best.

6. Your expectations and goals from this work
Have a look back at what you wrote about your expectations in Chapter 3.

(a) Did you get what you expected/hoped from the work in this book?
(b) How do you currently see your goals for your spiritual journey? Do they differ from what you laid out in Chapter 3?

Meditation

Review your experiences with meditation over this course. Did you experience greater "depth" in your meditation when you concentrated on one technique for several weeks? What problems did you encounter (e.g., maintaining regular practice)? What benefits did you gain? What is the next step for you?

Part Three

Release from Suffering

12 | Release from Suffering

I've given this last chapter a rather dramatic title, echoing the teachings of the Buddha and other spiritual leaders. What we are all seeking, in the end, is release from the various kinds of conflict associated with living—suffering that presents itself in extreme form when a serious disease is diagnosed. Our first thought when told we have cancer may be "I just want it to disappear and to have my life back as it was," but as time passes we may identify an even more fundamental wish: for peace of mind. The spiritual search is for peace, love, and experience of meaning, a state of mind that may bring physical healing, although it is not guaranteed to do so. One of our patients, expressed it in the following way:

> * *I think one of the most positive effects of my spiritual work is that it has broadened my view of what healing means, to one that goes beyond physical healing. Because the course of my illness is quite uncertain, I find that having a goal of physical recovery isn't enough. Certainly I hope for physical recovery, but realize that the extent and time span of this recovery are unknown, and may be less than I would ideally like . . . I find I am beginning to be able to let go of my*

sadness and anger about the uncertainty of my future when I am able to think of healing in a broader sense, which includes emotional and spiritual healing.

What we find as we undertake psycho-spiritual work

Have a look back now over the work we have done in Chapters 3 to 11 and try to fit it into a general scheme of psycho-spiritual healing.

You will have noticed how much of the work has been psychological in nature: we examined our pervasive habits of judging or condemning other people, and our usual dissatisfaction with conditions around us generally. Then we looked at self-judgment, which leads to guilt, although this is often unconscious. To protect ourselves against the pain of self-criticism and to absolve ourselves from responsibility for creating our own experience, we use various defenses: blaming and projection, developing an exaggerated sense of self-importance, and a preoccupation with personal desires.

To see the validity of this rather grim picture, it is quite essential to do our own self-study. I have found, in myself and in therapeutic work with hundreds of people, that most of us are only dimly aware of these mental processes at first. Many would claim, on first contact with these ideas, that they do not judge or doubt themselves, and that their problems are all the result of events beyond their control. We become familiar with our minds only when we go through a process of disciplined introspection.

Orthodox psychotherapy deals, of course, with most of these habits and perceptions, the usual aim being to help people strengthen their sense of self-worth, and to guide them toward healthier interactions with others. The spiritual journey has an additional, and much deeper, ultimate purpose: to discover, or uncover, the real self behind these habitual psychological patterns. If spiritual growth is our aim, however, it is not enough simply to meditate, or read spiritual texts. We need to do the psychological work first, because when we are locked into self-interest and self-protection we cannot connect spiritually—there is little "room" for apprehending the more subtle Divine Order, which is drowned out by our internal chatter (we are familiar with an analogous phenomenon at the social level—some people are so wrapped up in their own affairs, or their own thinking, that they have little ability to attend to what others want or say.)

How do the psychological and spiritual tasks fit together?

The diagram below (Figure 12.1) is a simple picture of the whole process. According to the spiritual view, our core problem arises from our separation from the Divine Source. This has led to the

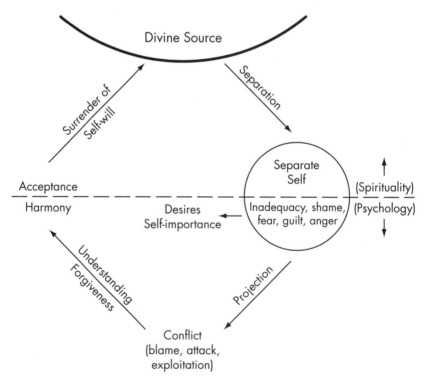

Figure 12.1
Consequences of separation and the process of healing.

distorted self-image and defensive patterns that we have been examining, and these habits in turn reinforce the separation. As supposedly separate beings, each the assumed center of his or her own universe, conflict with others is inevitable. The right-hand side of the diagram shows this process of separation and subsequent disharmony. I have described those events above the horizontal midline as "spiritual" because conventional psychology does not recognize separation from the Divine as a primary cause of dysfunction.

The left-hand side of the diagram shows the process of healing, first in psychological and then spiritual terms. We aim to regain connectedness. We practice first in areas familiar to conventional psychology: forgiveness or acceptance of other people, leading to the central task of accepting ourselves. The path becomes specifically spiritual when we begin to focus on fostering an ever-stronger connection with the Divine, through gradual diminishing of self-will, seeking guidance, and trying to be a "channel" for or witness to the unconditional love that grows in strength within us. Eventually, we need to adjust our lives according to our growing understanding of what we are meant to be and do. As we learn that we are a part of a larger whole, we see that we can choose to direct that part of it that we access toward helping or healing, rather than towards protecting our separateness, and competing with or exploiting others.

All phases of this work demand attention and effort—there is no escaping this fact, and any system of psychological or spiritual healing that professes to offer an easy way is inauthentic and misleading. In particular, the concept of surrender or non-attachment, alluded to in Chapter 9, is often difficult for the Western person, who has been trained from birth to assert his or her individual will. The concept is often misunderstood. To reiterate, it is not a passive or resigned acceptance, but a willingness to downplay our egocentric desires in favor of conformity with a much greater wisdom; to "hand over" our care to the Divine. Another way to practice surrender or acceptance, as explained by Eckhart Tolle in his wonderful book *The Power of Now*, is to attend fully to the present moment, instead of thinking constantly of past or future events. It does not mean being inactive. On the contrary, we need to be intensely active in our self-management, and we may choose to live very active lives, not for self-gratification, but in a spirit of service to the Divine and to others. Trust is required.

> ** I think that I have developed a stronger trust in God in the past year. . . . Initially I felt overwhelmed by the news [of metastatic spread, but] by the time I was ready to go to bed I was able to calm down, and I did this by reminding myself that I could accept whatever happened, that it is God's will, and I could pray for strength and peace of mind. As I've intensified my daily prayer, I have felt relief from these initial feelings of panic.*

Metaphors can aid understanding. The state of mind commended by spiritual masters could be likened to that of an employee dedicated to the service of his company or institution. The good employee learns to listen closely to what he or she is meant to do, and seeks guidance, rather than pushing a private agenda. Or another image: getting connected spiritually is like tuning our mental radio, avoiding the static, and centering in on the beautiful music that is available on certain stations. We find out what the universe wants of us by paying close attention, using the practices we have learned: meditation, prayer, devotion to a spiritual symbol like Christ, Krishna, or the Buddha, practicing non-judgment, releasing guilt, and reading and reflecting on the writings of the spiritual masters.

What is "mind"?

As the requirements of the spiritual journey become clearer to us, a number of questions may arise. "Will I lose my identity if I 'return to the Divine Source'?" "What must I give up?" "Will this work heal my body?" "If not, is it all worth the effort?" "Does some part of me survive the death of the body?" "What is my mind?" and, eventually, "Who am I anyway?" First, we will discuss "mind." In the following sections, we will ask how concepts of mind inform the question of possible effects of mind on body.

The nature of mind and its relationship to brain and body are issues that have been debated by philosophers for millennia. While this is not the place to enter that debate, we may note that there have been two main streams of thinking in the discourse. The first is realism, as exemplified by current scientific material- ism: the idea that mind is simply a by-product of brain function. The kidneys produce urine, the brain produces sensations and thoughts. This seems to have validity—after all, it is clear that when the body dies, the brain stops functioning, and presumably thinking also stops.

The second stream in this area of philosophy is idealism, roughly speaking, the view that all we ever know, and can know, are ideas in our minds. Our concepts of the assumed external world are of our own devising. Eastern spiritual philosophies often appear to take this line of thought to an ultimate point, asserting that there is, in fact, no separate self (Buddhism), and that all we seem to experi- ence in the material world is an illusion (Hinduism). This is diffi- cult for most of us to accept. We wonder, for example, if other people are supposedly figments of our imagination.

Various efforts have been made to reconcile the different view- points that have grown up around these major themes, as philo- sophically oriented readers will know. Our task here is not to choose sides, but to find a way of thinking about our minds and about ourselves that allows for possible healing effects of mind on body and explains the range of experiences that people pursuing a spiritual path have described. In his book, *The Self-Aware Universe*, physicist Amit Goswami attempts to reconcile the findings of mod- ern quantum physics, which also contradict commonsense ideas, with the major schools of philosophy and Western psychology. To paraphrase and simplify his argument, he proposes (as have oth- ers) that we have a "small mind," which does depend on brain func-

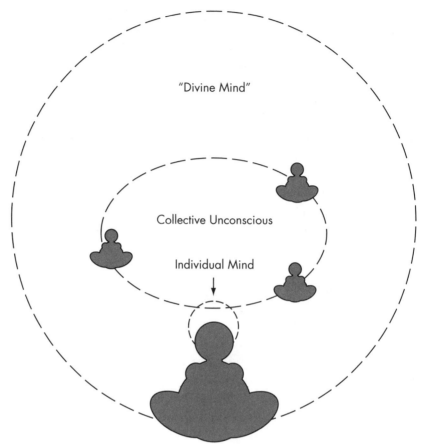

Figure 12.2
Levels of mind.

tion, and is largely conditioned by accumulated experiences to respond in ways that appear to obey the laws of classical physics. Then we also have a larger mind, or perhaps many levels of mind, that are not restricted to such classic (Newtonian) behavior.

The diagram above (Figure 12.2) may help us consider this. I have shown the small, individual mind as, indeed, an emanation from the brain. Extending beyond the body there may be further levels or shells of "mind." Although any definite subdivisions are likely to reflect simply our need to organize and control, we might propose a level of mind that extends across a species, embracing the minds of all humans, which could correspond to Jung's "collective unconscious." Beyond that, there may be still larger "minds" that include all living things, and eventually, the universe. The purpose of this simplistic model is to provide one way of organizing our experience as we pursue our meditation and strive to go beyond the restricted individual mind of brain-dependent thoughts.

What effects does "mind" have on body?

Now we can return to this pressing question with a broader perspective. First, let's consider the individual mind (product of the brain), whose existence is accepted by all, even the most materialistically oriented. It has significant effects on the body. Apart from the obvious control we have over our movements, we can also readily detect the impact of our thoughts and emotions on many functions that normally proceed unnoticed, such as blood pressure regulation, gastrointestinal functioning, patterns of breathing, and so on. These effects extend to influence over systems of the body that may be important in regulating some cancers, such as the immune system, that in the past were thought to be entirely beyond mental influence. Research in biofeedback, hypnosis, and psychosomatic medicine also shows that voluntary control can be achieved over other apparently independent functions of the body. For example, some individuals have the ability to arrest bleeding at will; wound healing, and recovery from surgery, can be accelerated by mental imaging and related techniques; and the experience of physical pain can be dramatically modified by mental techniques, as can the emotional pain of anxiety and depression. Thus without proposing anything esoteric we are aware that there is at our disposal an immensely powerful tool for improving life and health. It is tragic that our health-care system, reflecting the wishes of our society, has barely begun to incorporate well-researched mental self-control strategies into management of disease.

If the abilities of this everyday mind are not enough to satisfy us, we can draw on the expanded model in the "Levels of Mind" diagram to forecast mind-body potentials that lie beyond the realms of Newtonian physics and take on some of the aura and mystery of the quantum realm, where particles are moulded by the process of observing them, causally related events occur instantaneously, and time is no longer the reliable straight arrow we have come to depend on in our ordinary lives. I would suggest that these unusual potentials may become actualized when we make contact with, become aware of, or otherwise activate the higher, more all-encompassing levels of mind. I would further speculate that enhanced healing is possible with such contact. The ordinary rules by which material objects, including our bodies, seem to operate may be overridden under some circumstances by contact with these higher levels of mind. Currently we don't know how to measure such potentials directly, but any unbiased person who has looked at the evidence will acknowledge effects that are inexplicable by classical physical laws. For example, extensive and rigorous research has shown the capacity of mind to influence the proportion of pluses and minuses produced by a random number generator (see the account by Jahn and Dunne, referred to in the Reading List). I have personally experienced undeniable episodes of precognition and telepathy, and many patients have related to me their out-of-body episodes. Various authors have collected accounts of near-death experiences, which show many similarities to one another. (See, for example, *A Farther Shore*, by Yvonne Kason, a physician who had her own remarkable instance of rescue from an apparently fatal accident and who has collected and classified "spiritually transformative experiences" related to her by patients in her clinical practice.) We might also ask how to comprehend intense experiences of loving unconditionally and being loved, sudden feelings of connectedness, the "scales dropping from the eyes," as well as unexpected recoveries from serious disease that appear to contradict what we understand to be possible in our normal world.

How can we access our spiritual potential?

If these potentials exist, why are they not regularly available to us? Because we are so preoccupied with the chaos of our individual, "small mind" thinking. This is also why, as all of the great spiritual traditions tell us, we are seldom in contact with the Divine Order— our thinking, our egocentricity, gets in the way. A typical attitude was expressed clearly and honestly by one of our patients:

> * *I'm not going to be a new person. . . . I don't have any faith in the process. I am far from unhappy with my current balance of mind and spirit, so why change what works quite well?*

Our true nature is not primarily material—we are part of God or the Divine or the Tao. We are, in our essence, mind—not "small mind" but infinite mind. Our task is to experience this identity. It is here that the healing and spiritual journeys coincide. The route to healing lies through quietening our ego-chatter, and intensely seeking this connection with our "higher self." Perhaps, following Goswami and the idealist tradition, it may be that by the very act of seeking, we create form out of formless potential. God has been conceived of as having form or being without form. The choice would seem to be ours. Perhaps the intensity of our longing for connection, and our surrender (of the ego), draws out of the formless domain visions, angels, long-dead avatars, and sometimes changes in the material world, such as remarkable healings.

It is arrogant to suppose that our current ideas about reality, ideas peculiar to a particular biology and culture, have any absolute validity. We can, however, focus on our experience, and in practical terms, this is what matters. Models or theories about the nature of mind are simply aids to obtaining experience that will help us. My suggestion to people contemplating spiritual practice as a route to healing would be to read widely, find a spiritual tradition that suits you, an enlightened teacher if possible, and a way of conceptualizing the Divine that appeals; then having gained some control over your thinking, pursue meditation, prayer, or related techniques with all the intensity that you can muster. If you can find a supportive group of people with similar interests, that can be enormously helpful. If you feel devotion to an avatar like Christ or the Buddha, and like to see that figure in physical form, by all means use that route. If, on the other hand, you are deterred by some of the trappings of religion, think instead of the Divine as a formless intelligence or pervasive order to which you can "tune in." Or use both or many ways of thinking about it.

Should we seek "meaning" in cancer?

The "meaning" of cancer, or of any event, is far more than what is usually intended by the word, which is cause or consequence. It is, rather, the relationship of that event to everything else. The meaning we attribute to events depends on our understanding and awareness of the interconnectedness of things. The broader our understanding, the more connection we will find.

Healing is closely related to finding of meaning. Like understanding, healing can be at multiple levels, thus providing many potential points of control. If we are engaged in seeking meaning in our lives through the spiritual search, then we will address the possible meaning of our disease in these terms, and may be able to invoke a degree of healing through this level, which in no way denies the fact that the disease has biological determinants as well. We find, as we search, that cancer is connected to everything else in our lives, and that it may be affected by what we do in all other domains, particularly the spiritual. We come to understand that the healing journey is, in fact, a search for our true nature, our identity. It is very sad to note the prevalent societal view that "fighting" a disease simply means denying its likely effects, when the crisis offers such an incentive to probe more deeply into existential questions.

For many people, there is an excitement in becoming engaged in no less a task than uncovering our identity, who we are in relation to everything else in our world. It is the bold claim of the mystics that we can actually learn this through spiritual practice. In more mundane terms, as we progress spiritually we enjoy much more loving relationships with others, feel more secure, fulfilled, and more in tune with our world.

> * *I now don't have any doubts whatsoever, it's almost like I've been given a new brain, I have never felt so strongly about something before. No matter what I think about or read about, I always (most times) find something positive about the situation, usually relating to God's plan. I am truly thankful for my strong faith.*

One of our patients, initially said:

> *I can't see myself moving into a spiritual path per se . . . people are just imagining these things.*

However, after some months in a therapy group emphasizing spirituality, she told us that:

> *A presence is entering my meditations and is giving me a stillness I've not had before . . . and it is very clear to me that I am part of God.*

I have heard or read similar statements from many patients—that as a result of their psychological and spiritual work they have attained a peacefulness, joy, and sense of meaning greater than they have ever known, even in the face of dire medical predictions. Good experiences like this help us to keep going, but at every stage of our journey we are faced with the decision whether to push ahead or stop trying to grow, and either remain on a "plateau" or relapse into our previous habits. The dilemma becomes particularly acute if, despite our efforts, we have a disease that keeps progressing. People may become disillusioned and stop working under such conditions. They also frequently stop when their disease goes into remission! We are more inclined to continue as we learn to focus on personal and spiritual development for its own sake, leaving the physical outcome to the Divine.

A word to health-care professionals

Professionals sometimes argue that it is unfair to suggest that mind, let alone spirit, might affect something as concrete as a cancer. I think the reverse argument can be made with even more justification, that it is unfair, disempowering, to rule out possible mind-body effects, and thus deny people the opportunity to help themselves. However, we avoid this polarizing debate if we recognize that *our potential to use our various dimensions in the service of healing depends directly on our awareness of and connection with these levels of our being.* To the degree that we are connected spiritually, we will be able to invoke healing at this level. We cannot expect to relate our spiritual state to either mental or physical health until we have awareness of such a connection. Once we know it from personal experience, then we can use it. It is not a matter of adopting a belief uncritically, but of seeking our own understanding and experience, and using this to guide our actions. From this viewpoint, the clinical task is largely an educational one.

Understanding brings responsibility ("response-ability") for our own health. We have the obligation, I would submit, to take responsibility for maintaining our spiritual and mental state in accordance with our understanding. This is a sensitive issue. It is obviously not fair, or helpful, to blame ourselves or other people for failing to change what we see no rationale for changing. The appropriate course of action is to educate ourselves. However, there is a gradual growth of awareness in our culture of the many factors contributing to health and illness, and this awareness is improving our ability to respond at levels other than the physical. For example, almost everyone now understands that smoking promotes lung cancer and other diseases, which was not the case fifty years ago. Thus we now have a responsibility to discourage smoking, which we could not assume in an earlier time. More recently, there is a developing understanding of more subtle relationships between patterns of thought, such as continued judgmentalism and resentment, and heart disease. In time, we may come to see management of thoughts as being even more fundamental to maintaining health than good physical habits.

A final word to people with cancer

One might ask, why struggle to stay alive as a separate being if there is an all-encompassing realm to which we will ultimately return? This question becomes particularly poignant in the late stages of disease, when patients may ask "Should I continue to fight, or should I accept dying now?" There does come a time when it is appropriate to stop striving, and to allow the body to die. Meanwhile, while we are alive and able to act, is the spiritual search worth the effort? Well, I hope that what has been said in this book, and particularly the words of our patients that I've reported here, will convince you of the power of spiritual searching to bring peace. In terms of effects on physical healing you have read the view that, in the same way as for psychological and social dimensions (see Figure 2.2), making changes at the spiritual level will have the power to normalize biological processes, acting at least in part through the mind. We have the clinical observations of many therapists that people with cancer who become very involved with their psychological and spiritual work tend to live longer than predicted. Our own experiment, described in Chapter 1, is a systematic study of this phenomenon in a rigorous way; it requires confirmation by others, however. Also, it is difficult to separate the spiritual from the psychological work in such observations.

To relate some of my personal experience: after surgery for a serious colon cancer in 1987, my spiritual teacher Swami Radha wrote, "Don't do what you want; do what you ought!" This made perfect sense to me, and I intensified my spiritual seeking as a result. I went to an ashram (a center for psychological and spiritual growth), where I worked on my psychological problems and spiritual development, all day and every day, for three months. I was in a group with individuals training to be teachers of yoga, and our teachers were more advanced spiritual seekers. My spiritual work at the ashram, and subsequently, included wonderful instances of loving guidance, which continue to this day whenever I remember to "tune in." Thus I have personally no doubt about the constant availability of help from a transcendent or Divine source. Such a course might sound like an investment of time and money beyond what most can contemplate, but I believe something similar could be undertaken by many people, if they had sufficient belief in the power of such relatively intensive study to help them.

The theatre of action for self-help in healing is your own mind. Determination and work are required: I hope I haven't discouraged you by harping on this theme, but it would be irresponsible to say otherwise, however appealing a message of simple, magical cures might be. Don't become locked into a victim role by endlessly reviewing the horror story of your experience of cancer. Instead, resolve to take an active course, doing whatever you understand as having healing potential. Healing needs to become the top priority in your life, which means letting go of some other agendas. Once we have accepted the possibility that there is a transcendent dimension or Divine Power with the ability to help us, the work is, as we've discussed, mainly finding and diminishing our blocks to experience of this dimension. If we ask for help in the spiritual realm, meaning that we open ourselves to the higher dimensions of our own minds, we will find that help and support are abundantly available. Then having done what we can, we accept the outcome. Whatever it may be, biologically speaking, this course of action brings peace.

I wish you all understanding, joy, and healing on your path.

Main elements in the process of healing

Starting state	Process of healing	Healed state
1 What is reality, and how do I fit in?		
Matter is everything; comfort is primary goal; doubt, scepticism about a Divine Order	Reading scripture; discussion; meditation, reflection; open-mindedness	Mind is everything; seeking Divine guidance in all things; finding meaning is primary goal
2 Self-concept		
Separateness: self as central; fear; personal inadequacy; need to defend against all	Examining and dropping guilt, fear, specialness, entitlement	Self identified as part of the Divine Mind; non-attachment to body and world
3 Relationship		
Judgment and exploitation of others	Forgiveness, undoing the judgment	Acceptance, unconditional love; service to others
4 Projecting and extending		
Others blamed for all problems; projection of own guilt and fear	Examining and undoing projection; extending love	Extending love and compassion to all; knowing one is loved
5 Nurturing ourselves		
Driven by desires and self-will; unaware of true needs	Taking responsibility; aligning actions with needs	Simplicity, dedication to living a more spiritual life
6 Overall		
Unexamined life (mechanical, automatic)	Shaping of life according to goals	Constant maintenance of spiritual awareness; worship

Reading List

General Cancer Self-Help

Cunningham, A. J. *The Healing Journey*. Toronto: Key Porter Books, 2nd edition, 2000. (Forerunner to the present book.)

Cunningham, A. J. *Helping Yourself*. Toronto: Canadian Cancer Society. (A workbook and two audiotapes that can be obtained from the Canadian Cancer Society, 10 Alcorn St., Suite 200, Toronto, M4V 3B1.)

Elliott, R. E. *Dancing with Cancer: A Healing through Visualisation*. Dallas: Noteman Press, 1995. (A remarkable account of one patient's healing visualizations.)

Epstein, A. H. *Mind, Fantasy, and Healing*. New York, Delacorte Press, 1989. (A fascinating account of the dedicated use of imagery for healing).

Healing Journey Web site: «www.healingjourney.toronto.on.ca.» (This site provides information about the Healing Journey program as conducted in Toronto at the Princess Margaret Hospital.)

Simonton, O. C., Mathews-Simonton, S. and Creighton, J. L. *Getting Well Again*. New York, Bantam Books. (A very well-known early guide, emphasizing imaging.)

Other Psychological Self-Help

Achterberg, J. *Imagery in Healing: Shamanism and Modern Medicine*. Boston, Shambhala, 1985. (One of several fine books by Dr Achterberg on the subject of imagery.)

Assagioli, R. *Psychosynthesis*. New York, Penguin 1965, 1986. (An influential blend of modern psychology and traditional spiritual methods.)

Dossey, L. *Healing Words: The Power of Prayer and the Practice of Medicine*. San Francisco: Harper, 1993. (A comprehensive book by a physician on the relationship between prayer and healing.)

Burns, D. *Feeling Good: The New Mood Therapy*. Hearst, 1992. (An excellent guide to thought changing.)

Jampolsky, G. G. *Love Is Letting Go of Fear*. New York: Bantam Books, 1979. (Very simple and clear; beginning steps in adopting psychological change for spiritual purposes.)

Jampolsky, G. G. *Goodbye to Guilt*. New York: Bantam Books, 1985. (A very clear exposition, based on Jampolsky's study of *A Course in Miracles*.)

Rossman, M. L. *Guided Imagery for Self-Healing*. Tiburon, Calif.: H. J. Kramer, 2000. (An authoritative guide to the use of mental imagery.)

Meditation

Easwaran, E. *Meditation*. Petulama, Calif.: Nilgiri Press, 1978 (Simple and excellent.)

Easwaran, E. *God Makes the Rivers to Flow*. Tomales, Calif.: Nilgiri Press, 1991. (A collection of passages for meditative reading, selected and explained by the Eknath Easwaran, a modern spiritual master.)

Gawler, I. *Meditation. Pure and Simple*. Melbourne: Hill of Content, 1996. (A simple and excellent guide on meditation.)

Hahn, T. N. *The Miracle of Mindfulness*. Boston: Beacon Press, 1976. (A simple, profound book on self-awareness by a Buddhist master. Hahn has many similar books.)

Kabat-Zinn, J. *Full Catastrophe Living*. New York: Delacorte Press, 1990. (A comprehensive account of the use of awareness and meditation for healing.)

Kabat-Zinn, J. *Wherever You Go, There You Are*. New York: Hyperion, 1994. (A follow-up to *Full Catastrophe Living*.)

LeShan, L. *How to Meditate*. New York: Bantam Books, 1974. (Practical advice from a psychologist who has been a pioneer in cancer self-help.)

Radha, Swami S. *Mantras, Words of Power*. Kootenay Bay: Timeless Books, 1980. (The use of mantra for meditation by a modern spiritual master.)

Extending Our Ideas of Reality; the Paranormal

Goswami, A. *The Self-Aware Universe*. New York: J.P. Tarcher/Putnam, 1993. (A scientist explains how consciousness creates the material world.)

Jahn, R. G. and Dunne, B. J. *Margins of Reality*. San Diego: Harcourt Brace, 1987. (A very accessible account of a long and thorough program of paranormal research, and speculations on an expanded view of "reality.")

Kason, Y. *A Farther Shore*. Toronto: Harper Collins, 1994. (An account of near-death and other spiritual experiences in the lives of the author, a physician, and of patients in her practice.)

Spirituality

A Course in Miracles, Foundation for Inner Peace and Viking Books New York, 1975, 1996. (A truly remarkable book for the dedicated seeker. Includes daily lessons to deepen spiritual awareness.)

Berke, D. *The Gentle Smile*. New York: Crossroad, 1995. (As the title indicates, a wonderfully gentle account of bringing compassion into everyday life; based on the *Course in Miracles*.)

Bynner, W. (translator). *The Way of Life (the Tao Te Ching)*. New York: Capricorn Books, 1962. (Very many translations exist of this beautiful, classic, sixth-century Chinese text by Laotzu [or Lao Tso].)

Easwaran, E. *The Undiscovered Country: Exploring the Promise of Death*. Tomales Calif.: Nilgiri Press, 1996. (A spiritual approach to learning more from death; like all of Easwaran's books, beautifully written and highly accessible.)

Easwaran, E. *Original Goodness*. Berkeley, Calif.: Nilgiri Press, 1996. (My personal favorite among Eswaran's many wonderful books.)

Happold, F. C. *Mysticism*. New York: Penguin, 1981. (Contains a good general discussion of the subject and many first-hand accounts of spiritual experiences.)

Huxley, A. *The Perennial Philosophy.* New York: Harper and Row, 1970. (A classical account of the ideas underlying all religion; a good starting point for the thoughtful beginner.)

Kornfield, J. *A Path with Heart.* New York: Bantam Books, 1993. (A book on the spiritual journey by a well-known Buddhist thinker and writer.)

Krishnamurti, J. *Krishnamurti's Notebook.* New York: Harper and Row, 1976. Krishnamurti is a modern spiritual prophet who has written many books; this one is a diary of his personal reflections.

Lawrence, B. *The Practice of the Presence of God.* Mount Vernon, N.Y.: Peter Pauper Press, 1963. (A Christian classic.)

Levine, S. *A Year to Live. How to Live This Year As If It Were Your Last.* New York: Bell Tower, 1997. (Exactly as it says; doing the exercise.)

Levine, S. *Healing into Life and Death.* Garden City, New York: Anchor Press, Doubleday, 1987. (Levine's books bear the stamp of his own profound development.)

Mascaro, J. (translator). *The Dhammapada.* London: Penguin Books, 1973. (The classic, third-century Buddhist work on the path of liberation, love, life, and the will of God.)

Mascaro, J. (translator). *The Bhagavad Gita.* London: Penguin Books, 1988. (A recommended translation of this timeless Indian classic spiritual work.)

Merton, L. T. *Contemplative Prayer.* New York: Doubleday, 1971. (One of many fine books by an eloquent, modern Christian monastic.)

Peers, E. A. (translator). *The Way of Perfection: Teresa of Avila.* New York: Doubleday, 1991. (A translation of writings of the great, sixteenth-century Christian mystic.)

Pine-Coffin, R. S. (translator). *Saint Augustine, Confessions.* London: Penguin, 1961. (Many translations and editions of this classic work exist.)

Psychotherapy, and *The Song of Prayer* (supplements to *A Course in Miracles*). New York: Penguin, 1996. (Further channeled material from the source of *Course in Miracles.*)

Radha, Swami S. *Kundalini Yoga for the West.* Spokane: Timeless Books, 1978. (This monumental work is for the dedicated student who wishes to undertake personal spiritual growth from a yogic perspective.)

Radha, Swami S. *The Divine Light Invocation.* Spokane: Timeless Books, 1987. (Exercises leading up to the powerful invocation of light, as a symbol of spirituality.)

Tolle, E. *The Power of Now.* Vancouver: Namaste, 1997. (A living spiritual master describes a readily understandable route to the spiritual domain.)

Wapnick, K. *Talk Given on a Course in Miracles.* Roscoe, N.Y.: Foundation for "A Course in Miracles," 1989. (This is a very clear exposition of the main ideas of the course by its principal exponent.)

Yogananda, P. *God Talks with Arjuna; the Bhagavad Gita.* Los Angeles: Self-Realization Fellowship, 1995. (A monumental translation and exposition of the Indian classic, by a modern spiritual master, living in the West.)

Yogananda, P. *Autobiography of a Yogi.* Los Angeles: Self-Realization Fellowship. Twelfth edition, 1993. (A classical work; an account of the development of a spiritual master. Eminently readable.)

Zukav, G. *The Seat of the Soul.* New York: Fireside, 1989. (A fine simple account of the spiritualizing of everyday life.)

Index

Further materials on the Healing Journey

For more information on the Healing Journey, visit our Web site at «www.healingjourney.toronto.on.ca».

This book was preceded by *The Healing Journey* (Key Porter Books, 2000).

The *Helping Yourself* kit—a workbook and two audiotapes—contains the material for the first level of our courses. It can be obtained by writing to:

The Canadian Cancer Society
10 Alcorn Avenue
Suite 200
Toronto, Ontario,
M4V 3B1
Attention: Inventory Clerk

A package including six videotapes, two audiotapes, a workbook, and *The Healing Journey* will soon be available. It documents the first level of our course; the videos are a series of lessons and discussions between a group of cancer patients and Dr. Cunningham. Information can be obtained and orders placed through «www.worldhealthsites.com». This package is intended for private study or use by institutions as a teaching tool.